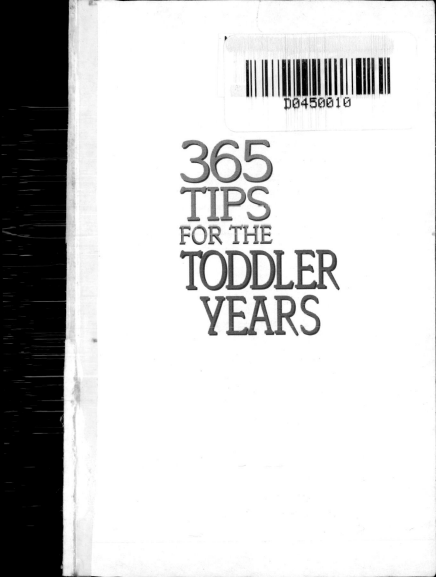

365
TIPS
FOR THE
TODDLER
YEARS

AGES 1 TO 3

365 TIPS FOR THE TODDLER YEARS

Julian Orenstein, M.D.

Author of *365 Tips for Baby's First Year*

Adams Media Corporation
Avon, Massachusetts

Published by
Adams Media Corporation
57 Littlefield Street, Avon, MA 02322 U.S.A.
www.adamsmedia.com

ISBN: 1-58062-563-0

Printed in Canada.

J I H G F E D C B A

Library of Congress Cataloging-in-Publication Data
Orenstein, Julian.
365 tips for toddler years / by Julian Orenstein.
p.   cm.
ISBN 1-58062-563-0
1. Toddlers. 2. Toddlers--Care. 3. Child rearing.
I. Title: Three hundred sixty-five tips for toddler years. II. Title.
HQ774.5 .O74   2001
649'.122--dc21   2001046304

This publication is designed to provide accurate and authoritative information with
regard to the subject matter covered. It is sold with the understanding that the publisher is not
engaged in rendering professional medical advice. If assistance is required, the services of a
competent professional person should be sought.

Many of the designations used by manufacturers and sellers to distinguish their products are
claimed as trademarks. Where those designations appear in this book and Adams Media was
aware of a trademark claim, the designations have been printed in initial capital letters.

Interior illustrations by Barry Littmann
Cover photo by Getty Images/Regine M.

This book is available at quantity discounts for bulk purchases.
For information, call 1-800-872-5627.

To Aunt Audrey and Aunt Shany,
a pair of fine moms
who shared a tip or two about their toddlers.

Contents

Read Together

Toilet Time

Grooming

Bedtime

Anger Management

About the Parents

About the Parents (continued)

Playing with Others

Hands Full?

The Dreaded "No"

Temper, Temper

Quality Family Time

Be Prepared . . .

Be Prepared . . . (continued)

Medicines

The Doctor Said . . .

The Doctor Said . . . (continued)

Healthy Habits

Toddler Habits

Drive-time Do's

Dental Do's

Things to Know

Things to Know (continued)

Heads Up!

Creative Crafts

Communication

Communication (continued)

Kitchen Capers

Discipline

Discipline (continued)

Bright Ideas

Scary Stuff

Playtime

Sun Safety

Shy Guy

Say "Cheese!"

It's My Party

On the Move

Daddy!

Zero Tolerance

Your Other Job

Introduction

> Nobody expects the Spanish Inquisition!
> Our chief weapon is surprise—surprise and
> fear . . . fear and surprise. Our *two* weapons
> are fear and surprise—and a ruthless efficiency
> . . . our *three* weapons are fear, surprise,
> ruthless efficiency and . . .
> —*Monty Python's Flying Circus*

A baby is born in a sweating, shrieking haze of hysteria that is somehow made okay by its final appearance. (If you're the mom, it's a thousand times worse.) A toddler, on the other hand, debuts stealthily in a mischievous burst of effort and concentration: plop! one foot down; pit-*pat!* the second foot lands; and it's off and running from there.

The quite substantial difference between these two appearances, aside from the obvious panic and confusion factor, is familiarity. When an important stranger arrives, you want to be ready and on your best behavior, but you're somehow caught a little short. When a neighbor drops in for a visit, a little disarray is not such a terrible thing. Your toddler has just emerged from the cocoon of your once-new baby; she sleeps in the same crib, wears the same outfits and giggles the same delicious giggle. At first, you might not even realize she is here. But make no mistake; there are big changes ahead.

For all the chaos and tumult of a baby's birth, the days and months that follow are tranquility itself. Oh, sure, there's crying and ear infections and baffling *snurrups* (inexplicable yet worrisome-looking baby doings that defy logical or medical explanation). But once you've been subjected to the tempest of an eighteen-month-old's fury over a lifeless, yet uncooperative, plastic toy, that first year is softened by a gauzy, rosy glow. *Trouble? What trouble? He was an angel when he was a baby! I don't know where this little hellion came from . . .*

We are all unprepared for the Spanish Inquisition. Let's use this analogy to explore the changes of toddlerhood.

Their chief weapon is fear. Once granted the gift of mobility, toddlers take advantage of quicksilver-like speed (especially in comparison to us lumbering achy-backed parents) to find the most poisonous speck in the yard, the sharpest stick to squint at, and the angriest dog in the park to teach it what happens when you yank its tail. Of course we're concerned with the vaguely encompassing, global fears for our baby's happiness, future, or Environment (capital E: ozone holes, arctic drilling, overpopulation), but that pales next to our fears of the hazards a toddler can plunge himself into *today*.

Their second weapon is surprise. Babies endlessly surprised us with their smiles, their newly awakened ability to sleep through the night or pull themselves into a stand. Nestled inside the safety of a play-table or fenced inside a play gate, a baby surprises you without inflicting harm on either you or him. Well, toddlers, too, are a font of surprise: new words and phrases, new problem-solving skills, newfound capabilities of sometimes helping mommy and daddy. A toddler masters the element of surprise by appearing in two places improbably quickly, if not, in fact, simultaneously. And once inside the mall's dumpster, he can find the discarded McDonald's fries mixed with rat poison, challenging you to cross twenty yards of other moms, strollers, and security guards to grab it from his hands before his teeth chomp shut. So perhaps the *quality* of surprise changes little from baby to toddler, but the *quantity* can leave you gasping. Literally.

Then we have their ruthless efficiency, and this is where a toddler really makes tremendous strides over any baby. Changing a baby's diaper and slipping on a new outfit took *maybe* two minutes in a well-oiled household, and then it's out the door and on to grandma's. A two-year-old can consume the better part of a morning on the same activity, all the while reducing you to a blubbering mess. A "no" here, a pouty sulk there; heels dig in for a screaming, wailing tantrum and when *that's* done and you think you're out the door, he trips you up once more by spilling the pasta salad you were taking along.

Not to put too fine a point on it, teaching the fine arts of taking turns with friends, recognizing household dangers, and eating a balanced diet requires a steady discipline and a very even temper. Your toddler's job is far simpler: Test out how much the Grownups really wants you to listen and play nicely. While superior force, and perhaps intelligence, is on your side, the sniper is having a far better time, risks be damned (living on the edge is always half the fun).

And last but not least: Among the weapons of the Spanish Inquisition is a fanatical devotion to the Pope. Babies smile and coo and fuss for mommy and daddy. You're their world, through and through. A toddler, though, gets signals from the Dog Star. Just watch an episode of Teletubbies and you'll see what I mean. Toddlers listen to an inner directive that insists they experiment with putting clothes on backwards, kicking frantically while being diapered, spraying out half-chewed peas in the restaurant even though you've already adopted that I've-had-it-up-to-here tone of voice. Sometimes there's no reaching them. The burgeoning cortex of your toddler's brain teems with signals, impulses, and desires, and he's busy tuning into the chatter and strange music emanating from station after station.

As you will see, toddlers are creatures wholly unlike the babies they'd once been. It's astounding that they should transfigure themselves with just a single step, but there it is. And if you think that's amazing, just wait. They all end up as *kids*.

Books about Friendship

One-year-olds aren't literary critics; their restless parents are. Children want to be entertained. The following, totally biased, nonrandom sample of books just happens to be one I know intimately, having seen them receive the ultimate accolade: "Again! Again!" These books teach the lesson of a single best friend, or a whole bunch of friends working together.

- *Elmer* (David McKee): A crazy-quilt elephant finds it tough to be the class clown. By leaving and returning in disguise, he discovers his valued, unique role in his community.
- *George and Martha* (James Marshall): Oversized hippos (sounds redundant, doesn't it?) who pick silly fights over bruised feelings, but work them out.
- *Rainbow Fish* (Marcus Pfister): A sparkly, glittery fish learns that sacrifice—giving up something important to you, not just what's unwanted and available—leads to respect and friendship.

TIP

Toilet Training: Everybody Ready?

No, they never just say, "Mom, can you teach me how to use the toilet? I'm ready now!" (Does your husband ever say: "Honey, keep your eyes peeled for the next gas station, I think I'm gonna need directions"?) Be alert for signs that work to your advantage. Staying dry is more an hour-to-hour phenomenon than having an unpooped diaper, so peeing in the bowl is usually mastered first. When she's ready to train, she may start doing the dancy-pants routine of hopping and grabbing when she has to go and is, for the first time, holding back a little. Ask her: Do you have to make a pee-pee? Do you want pull-ups? Do you want to be a big girl like [friend] [older sib]?

Be ready: have the time to sit (or stand) by the toilet for as many tries as it takes to produce a winner. Clear your calendar for a few days in order to seal the deal.

TIP

2

Toilet Training: Just Saying No

You've got the potty seat, the potty books, and there's a gleam in her eye because she's about to become a big girl like her best friend, Sara. Then all of a sudden the house of cards collapses. The light in her eyes dims; the fire in the belly, so to speak, burns out. She goes back to the corner to squat and grunt and won't even look at the bathroom. She could care less about the Rugrats temporary tattoos she herself picked out as a reward.

Forget it. The moment's gone; nothing you can do will make it come back. Bargain and reason with her if you must, just for the sake of trying, but don't get bent out of shape. Wait a few weeks; she'll try again. (Just don't plan a vacation that doesn't include diapers . . .)

TIP

3

Nail Trimming

Whether or not your twenty-month-old chooses out of the blue one day to make nail trimming an issue, it still must be done carefully and sensitively in order to avoid a death match.

Nails are softest after a bath, and bathing should have a mellowing effect, anyway. Sing a song or have him hold a book while you're doing his toes.

And do trim the toes first. He'll be a little distracted, plus they're less sensitive than fingers.

Use a clipper rather than scissors in case of any sudden wiggles.

When he starts squirming out of control, take a break, even if you're not done. A nail-trimming session requires cooperation.

TIP

4

Nap Schedules

Many textbooks on pediatrics contain a bar chart of children's sleep needs as they grow older. In a baby's first weeks and months, a few short bars are present, indicating wakeful moments in the midst of mostly uninterrupted sleep. By one year old, there are usually a couple of "sleep bars" in the middle of the day, lasting from one and a half to two and a half hours. Within half a year, you'll be down to one sleep bar for one to two and a half hours. This dwindles down to an hour by age two and a half to three, and then it vanishes in well over half of all toddlers.

Like most moms, you'll greet this development with a twinge of annoyance (there goes my morning break!). That will fade away rapidly: after all, this releases you from a roadblock in your daily doings. Pretty soon, you'll be fighting the bear he's become at what *used* to be naptime . . .

TIP

5

Getting Frustrated

An eighteen-month-old starts building with blocks by himself very nicely. But then out of the blue he swats at the tower he's just built and starts sobbing uncontrollably. When you ask him why and offer to help, he screams. Then he tries all over again. What the heck is going on?

At eighteen months, he may have a grand architectural scheme in mind, but the blocks just aren't cooperating. It doesn't look *right* to him. He may not know how to express this, just as he can't get his blocks to meet his expectations. By asking what he's building you may be able to get him to say what he's aiming for and, more important, open up about his frustration over how the toys are failing his expectations.

Have him break the job up into smaller, more manageable steps or get him to transition to a new activity if he has unrealistic expectations.

TIP

6

Exile from Paradise 1

W hen is it appropriate for a twenty-two-month-old to forgo the warmth of the family bed?

When it's time for you, as parents, to have "alone time." The loss of intimacy is a legitimate imposition on a normal family life. Let's frame it another way. You want your groove back, but it doesn't work when your partner feels inhibited by either the time constraints imposed by a dozing daughter or what is required to keep it quiet.

TIP

7

Exile from Paradise 2

How do I get my son out of my bed and into his own?

Well, there's the fast way and there's the slow way. The fast method is to announce that on a certain day—and make sure he understands exactly when—he's going into his own crib for good. You're asking him to give up a security object, so treat the matter carefully with him. On the given day, make sure he gets lots of bedtime stories and hugs, perhaps a new stuffed friend for the crib, and expect some tears.

The slow way involves letting him sleep in your bed, then moving him to the crib when he's asleep. Tell him ahead of time he'll wake up in his crib, and this is the way it will be for the next couple of weeks. After that, he starts off by going to sleep in the crib.

TIP

8

Miss Manners 1

Dear Miss Manners:

I'm a stay-at-home mom, but the rest of my friends work. Whenever one of their children is sick at preschool, or they get tied up in meetings and can't do a pick up, they turn to me. I always say yes, but here's the problem: I have a life and child of my own! Help!

Dear Patsy:

You're right; their problems aren't your responsibility. It's nice to be able to help a fellow mother, but, just as you do for your child, set expectations and reinforce limits. Other parents probably don't realize the effort this favor requires, especially if you've never let on that it's an imposition. Once you explain your boundaries, they'll understand, and they'll respect you for it. Just like your toddler does when you reinforce a rule that is, in fact, a rule.

TIP

Critic Buster

Children can be sublimely oblivious to their surroundings (oh, let's say when he's surrounded by a three-inch sea o' toy parts strewn merrily about, and Mom is planted squarely in his face telling him for the fifth time to clean up his mess or he gets no dessert tonight). But they can be overwhelmingly sensitive to the *sotto voce* comment from Aunt Rachel who casually observes, "Your children run around like wild maniacs."

Don't let others criticize your child—or your parenting skills—in front of him. This is as true for strangers as well as friends or relatives. Tell them that you appreciate their concern for your child's safety (or behavior, or whatever else the catty remark was directed toward) but that you try as hard as you can to ensure he's always behaving in a manner that's safe (or considerate or whatever).

Resist the temptation to return with a volley of your own: You never know who might happen to be a black-belt martial artist, after all.

TIP

10

Nursing in the Second Year

Consider this: If you're nursing your baby longer than six months, you're in limited company. Three out of four moms throw in the towel before the first birthday. You're also in good company. The American Academy of Pediatrics has women aim for a year, based, in part, on evidence that breastfeeding *women* benefit (lower risk of breast and ovarian cancer, osteoporosis, hip fractures) as well as their babies.

It's not easy. First and foremost, stick to your guns. Laws that criminalize public breastfeeding are going down one by one. The time to stop is when you and your child feel it's time to stop. Locally you may not feel a lot of support, but the worldwide average age of stopping breastfeeding is somewhere over four years.

If you and your child both lead busy lives, aim the nursing breaks for wake-up and nighttime "snack." If a midday feeding is part of the routine, the degree of difficulty goes up: you either have to work, or have day care, nearby. Scope out a place where you can be private (and maintain a little dignity) for the ten or fifteen minutes you'll need.

TIP

Bring music and a couple of sets of headphones to complete the tune-out process, and return to work refreshed.

11

Breastfeeding and Pregnancy

Women who breastfeed a child into toddlerhood and then become pregnant face a number of conflicts and discomforts. First, the nipples and breasts become sore from pregnancy. Your toddler will notice some involuntary withdrawal and irritability. Second, the hallmark symptom of the first trimester is fatigue. You won't have the energy you once did. Your milk supply may diminish in response to hormonal changes, and it may taste different. Your body's hormonal recalculations release something known as *oxytocin*, which can trigger painful uterine contractions while breastfeeding.

It ain't gonna be easy or fun. Not every woman experiences these changes, but be aware of them ahead of time. It may be time to wean, if you and your first child are ready, or it may take some figuring out how to keep the nursing going.

TIP

12

Know "No"? No, Not Yet

To internalize means to really, truly, honestly understand something with your left brain that your right brain accepts as a truth. Your twelve- to eighteen-month old is getting there with the concept of "no." He knows it means no, but hasn't yet internalized its true meaning. As a captive of his impulses, he knows that dumping the five-gallon Lego tank will get him in trouble, or that spilling the gallon of milk will get him in even bigger trouble. On one level, he knows Mommy always says "no" every time he starts to upend containers that ought not be upended. But that awareness is fifteen seconds behind the cerebral cortex telling the arms: Yeah! Do it now!

With time, he will learn to synchronize the impulsive and controlling parts of his brain. Until then, keep your cool. Don't get mad at him, don't explode, and don't worry. He's getting there, bit by bit.

TIP

13

Looking for Trouble

From the age of about one and a half to two and a half, he can't be responsible for his impulses. He has achieved a mindset akin to juvenile delinquents actively prowling around looking for trouble. Curiosity dictates his impulses before his conscience sets limits. He wants to see whether you (or the cat) are going to punish him for yanking the cat's tail.

A smart move, frankly. You're his constant companion; he knows you better than anyone else: he perceives your moods, tempo, and attention span daily. Hourly. And he sees you don't always act the same way in the same situation. He knows that even though you've said, "No means no," you don't always make it stick.

The result: For the space of a year or so, he'll test out which set of directives you really, always, absolutely stand by, and those that show chinks in the armor.

TIP

14

Fight It? Wimp Out?

We all pick our battles, and for good reason: situations differ. Sometimes your aim is to achieve better manners or a more balanced diet. Important stuff, but not as critical as, for instance, teaching her a stovetop is hot and can burn or that a street corner is a dangerous place that requires absolute control over happy feet. So when should you be flexible?

- Don't set yourself up for failure over a low-priority issue.
- Give in occasionally to taste preferences in clothing and food.
- Stand firm on safety: Toddlers don't play with knives. Toddlers hold hands crossing the streets. This is non-negotiable.
- When you give in, acknowledge that her victory was earned by being grown up enough for a new set of rules—and that means more responsibility.

TIP

15

Your Inner Child Wants to Throw a Tantrum

Your brain, modern science has discovered, is like the central control unit of HAL, the temperamental computer of the movie *2001*. That is, you have a series of buttons, and when they're pushed in sequence, you go haywire.

This is what your eighteen-month-old is doing when he continues to shriek and writhe when you're changing his diaper and you've already given three warnings to keep still. Now your inner child is ready for a tantrum. Here are ways to avoid it:

1. Stand back. Finish the diapering, and make an exit. Pop in a video to engage your child's attention, and disengage yourself before you melt down.
2. Have a snack if your blood sugar is running low. Put on fresh makeup. Listen to a favorite song with headphones on.
3. Restore your karma.

TIP

16

Remember: This is hard-wiring, it's not just you. You're a good parent. You are!

'N Sync 1

Just as short parents may have tall children, easygoing, laid-back parents may produce the toddler equivalent of Marilyn Manson.

Temperamental mismatches are not unusual, and can be terribly frustrating. When Laurie had her first child, her and her husband's intense mellowness became a roadblock to coping with the tornado that was their offspring. Assertiveness was a trait unknown to them, and unfortunately their philosophy—best summed up in the term "whatever!"—was thoroughly useless in disciplining their increasingly destructive son.

A few months of therapy later, they made the discovery ("Oh! Coo-o-o-o-l!") that asserting their parental judgment did not, in fact, mean anger with their son. It just meant that they had to enforce the rules. They lived happily, if chaotically, ever after.

TIP

'N Sync 2

In this end of the temperamental spectrum, consider the case of Terry, the focused mom, and dawdling Andy. Terry would beg and plead with Andy to finish breakfast, get dressed, and get in the car. He was in the Andy Zone, rearranging the magnet letters on the fridge while Terry was getting dressed and ready. She would, of course, lose it when she saw Andy had completed none of his tasks.

Terry can't hover over Andy every moment of the day, but on the other hand, no toddler follows instructions like a paid secretary. A pokey kid like this always needs frequent prompts and nudges in the right direction. Terry's strategy became to ping-pong back and forth between her own routines and one-minute drills: Three more mouthfuls! Shirt on! Coat on! Into the car by the time I count to ten! Without threatening tone or rising temper, the commands were issued with good humor and firmness. She emphasized she was counting on him to help follow the rules so he could get to his play date or preschool.

TIP

18

TeeVeeeeeee

How much TV is enough? Are people who banish TV *better* somehow? Does it become a substitute for effective parenting?

You can drive yourself to distraction by questioning TV's role in the life of your child. A few sanity clauses:

- It's as central to modern life as a car or refrigerator. It has its proper place.
- A half-hour each day is adequate, an hour and a half is too much. The time spent watching TV is time spent not exploring, burning energy, or socializing.
- The best time to sit in front of the TV is when your toddler is too tired for other activities.
- Until you know the shows she's watching, sit with her and gauge the content for age and developmental appropriateness.
- TV won't ruin her eyes.

TIP

19

Bead in the Nose: Redux

Many moons ago, I made the sage and weighty observation that upon finding a bead in a child's nostril, the responsible parent promptly seeks a doctor's assistance to relieve the obstruction.

Baah! Twentieth-century thinking!

The modern mommy can save the copay and time wasted in the waiting room by performing a simple, easy maneuver. Once you've discovered Barbie's missing pink slipper lodged firmly in the left side of little Mara's nose, you can confidently teach her a new "game." It's called "Mommy's gonna give wittle woogums a special kiss."

Lie her down on a firm surface, like the kitchen table. Cover the unobstructed nostril with a finger, have Mara open wide and plant your mouth firmly over hers. Then blow a short, strong breath as she inhales. It may take two or three tries, but the positive pressure can cleanly push out the object, or loosen it enough for you to readily pull it out. This works about 90 percent of the time, but if it hasn't budged after several tries, then it's on to the doc.

TIP

20

Making Sense of: Creams and Lotions

There's an old saying among dermatologists: If it's wet, dry it; if it's dry, wet it. But what if it itches as well? The top three itch lotions:

1. Antihistamine lotion (diphenhydramine, a.k.a. Benadryl, Caladryl, etc.): The active ingredient may actually be absorbed into the bloodstream from open skin. This occurs with sunburn, chicken pox, or poison ivy, the most common conditions for which the lotion is used. Plus, it causes a secondary irritation rash all by itself.

2. Calamine lotion: The active ingredient is calamine, combined with other protectants, like zinc oxide. It soothes skin irritated from poison ivy, sunburn, or bug bites. The downside: getting the thick, pasty crust off once it dries.

3. Moisturizing lotions: Emollients, which carry water in an oil emulsion, rehydrate dried keratin bonds (which causes flaking and itching). Babies need no aloe, scent, or additives.

TIP

21

Coping with Cuts

When cuts happen, who ya gonna call? A primary care doctor, pediatrician, or family doc may sew lacerations on a daily basis or she or he may have hung up the latex gloves years ago and defer to the ER or a plastic surgeon. When is a plastic surgeon likely to make a difference?

A simple, horizontal cut on the forehead, even on a future Miss America, can be fixed by anyone to yield a nearly invisible scar. (A noteworthy aside: the most durable skin layer is the "basement membrane." Any cut deeper than that exposes fat and leaves a permanent scar.)

Put yourself in the hands of a plastic surgeon when the cut has multiple branches, if there is significant contamination (larvae, cement, McDonald's), or if there is an underlying fracture or tendon injury. An honest doctor (or physician's assistant) will always tell you if he feels capable of mending the wound. If you have any doubts, ask him if he would fix the same cut on his own daughter.

Modern Miracles: Tissue Glue

Oh to be alive in the twenty-first century! Nowadays, some cuts need no stitching at all. In the late 1990s, the FDA gave a green light to tissue adhesive (glue), taking all the pain and fear out of one of toddlerhood's greater passages. But wait, it's not really a magic bullet. There are, don't you know, problems. Glue should only be used for small (under a centimeter), clean cuts. Any laceration that's gaping requires internal stitches, and dirty wounds or bites are not appropriate for glue. In fact, steri-strips can almost always fill in for glue. In some ways, tape is often better. The delicate forehead laceration, for example: Glue would be an ideal way to close it, only the liquid tends to run down into the eyelids, gluing them shut (and yes, I've spent hours trying to undo that mess! Talk about seething moms . . .)

Bottom line: Beware of anything labeled a "miracle" cure.

TIP

Sugar and Hyperactivity

Sugar does not cause hyperactivity. By hyperactivity, I mean the behavior syndrome known as ADHD, Attention-Deficit Hyperactivity Disorder. ADHD is a generalized, long-term problem with impulsiveness and inattention as well as overactivity. Sugar is, however, fuel. In the case of a zippy eighteen-month-old, this fuel can be rocket fuel. It provides energy for him to do the million and a half things he wants to do (all in the space of thirty minutes or so).

There is no good way for scientific scrutiny to distinguish between the normal abundance of exuberant energy of a one-year-old (who has a brief attention span) and an excessively energetic or inattentive one-year-old. Giving a high-octane toddler candy or cookies makes him "hyper" because you're providing him with play energy, but it will not, in the long term, push him into being a child who has problems with hyperactivity.

TIP

24

Nondairy Calcium Sources

Lactose-intolerant children need calcium as much as kids whose intestines aren't so picky, and with a little sleuthing you can get by just fine without any milk whatsoever. Where do you find calcium? First, try calcium and vitamin D–fortified soy milk. Most of the big juice makers (Tropicana, Minute Maid) offer calcium-fortified products as well. After that, you're on to fruits and grains. These ought be a good part of her diet anyway, so the daily minimum shouldn't be too far away.

The USDA makes free, user-friendly booklets detailing which foods to choose from. They're not just for calcium, but for any and all other minerals and nutrients that pass your son's or daughter's lips. Best find: beans and peas, because you can always use them in a chili.

TIP

25

Handling the Stalemate

With the suddenness of a thunderstorm in June, your happy little Pooh-bear may just go off the deep end while having a grand play date with her best friend, Amber. Said best friend may become the sworn enemy if she grabs for the toy your child wanted to use at that exact same moment. If Pooh-bear's not playing fairly, let Amber have the toy and stand your ground.

Once Pooh-bear escalates to an all-out hissy fit, just walk out on her. If she's barking "no!" complete with tears, at your efforts to intervene, just give up after a few good tries. Send her to a quiet place, let Amber play with the toy, and wait out the storm. Calm weather usually follows—at least for a little while.

TIP

26

Thumb-Sucking Blues

Thumb sucking: a trait desirable in a six-week-old and anything *but* desirable in a six-year-old. Up until the age of four or so, it is a common behavior more akin to a security blanket than a bad habit.

During iffy situations, some children withdraw into the comfort of a thumb in the mouth. But it's got to stop *sometime* since there are a few consequences. On the minor side, thumb sucking causes blisters or impetigo. On the major side, misaligned teeth and possibly even social stigmatization in preschool or kindergarten can result.

Look for your best chance to divert this behavior in other directions without making a big stink about it. Take advantage of his willingness to give it up when, for example, he develops a sore from sucking, or is entering or returning to school. Offer stickers, or chart his progress to build up rewards. Provide bulky, colorful bandages if that entices him.

TIP

27

Curbing Road Rage

There may be a few guys for whom this applies, but this is almost purely a mom thing. (Guys, back me up on this!) When little Tucker is tucked safely and securely into the back seat and a big jerk in front of you cuts you off unexpectedly, the last thing you should do is let go with a string of furious profanities. Your little tape recorder in the back seat will replay them, word for word, in front of the worst possible audience: your mom, your mother-in-law, your parole officer. Long before this happens, pick out a phrase or a term that will not only let you vent your anger, but can stand endless repetition in front of any audience. Words with a *k* are satisfying. Try these:

- "Nose picker!"
- "Did you see what that cake eater just did?!"
- "That bonehead coulda gotten us all killed!"

TIP

28

Let Her Read to You

Kids learn their books word for word. Try to skip a page from a reading of "One fish, two fish" (as I have done—and don't recommend) and you'll hear about it! If you find yourself dozing off during the seventh week of nothin'-but-Tom-Kitten (as I have also done), let her read to you. This is actually a sweet way to hear how you sound to her, since you'll get every inflection back, syllable for syllable. A "fiction reading" also makes for a great video moment.

TIP

29

Family Game Night

Dad works, Mom works. Dad gets home late, Mom gets home late. If only it ended there. Neighborhood and community obligations, catching up with bills, and other routine responsibilities chew the weeks up fast. In your weekly time budget, set aside one night a week for family, and make it an inviolable commitment.

Whatever game you play—dolls, puppet show, board games—you're guaranteed to find it more satisfying than any other duty. Anyone competing for your time who doesn't respect the sanctity of this night can go rot. The sooner you start, the sooner it becomes a part of your family life.

TIP

30

Nathan's Car Game

Long trips require a new activity every ten to fifteen minutes. Our son Nathan made up this game when he was five, but it works great for kids as young as two. Everyone in the car gets assigned a color. When your color car passes you, you score a point. Trucks don't count because the cab and trailer are usually different colors, and this causes unnecessary confusion and arguments. The car can't just be visible from the window—it has to actually pass you to count. Five points wins. Keep the game short to maintain interest, and start a new round if your toddler hasn't grown bored.

With a little luck, this will also get you to slow down a little on highways; if you find you're passing all the cars, you're probably above the speed limit.

TIP

31

Wallace and Gromit

The most exceptionally endearing creatures ever to grace the small screen are Wallace and Gromit. Nick Park's claymation creatures are worth the money and withstand repeated viewings. The British Wallace, an inventor, faces age-old dilemmas: finding love, protecting his family, where to go "on holiday." He solves this last riddle in a particularly memorable way: "That's it, Gromit, we'll go where there's cheese!"

Gromit, his dog, never barks or even growls, but his enormously expressive face speaks eloquently and compellingly. Months after our own children had tired of them (in favor of the irritating Pokémon and Powerpuff Girls abominations), I was begging them for one more viewing of *A Close Shave* or *A Grand Day Out*.

With luck, the three episodes will soon be joined by more. Legions are waiting.

Instant Book

If your son's favorite book is not immediately available on demand, there's a sly way to short-circuit a tantrum or head off hysterics. Press your hands together; then spread them out, side by side. Start to "read." You have undoubtedly memorized: "In the great green room . . ." Wiggle your fingers on one hand for each page, and within a page or two he will pick up the story himself. If you haven't completely committed the text to memory (or stumble over a word or two as it rolls out from rote repetition), fear not. He'll tell you exactly where you are. This is better than e-books on a Palm computer. Your hands can become any book without ever paying for a single download.

Midnight Caller

What do you do when a stubborn two-year-old stands over you at two in the morning demanding a bottle? You gird your loins for battle.

Every response carries a price, but some are less costly than others. Giving in to her in the short term sets you up for sleepless nights in the long term. Sorry to say, your best chance of permanent victory makes for some awful nights in the meantime.

Unless she has a real problem that needs fixing—vomiting in bed, for example—say no and, if need be, gate her inside her room. She's just exploring another way to test limits. Ignore her for as long as you can, even if it means waking the entire family. This, too, shall pass.

TIP

34

Modern Miracles: Lactose Intolerance Test

Lactose intolerance is deficiency of the enzyme lactase, which breaks down the milk sugar lactose for absorption into the bloodstream. It's not a true "allergy" to milk. Common symptoms are nausea, cramps, bloating, and diarrhea, starting a half-hour to two hours after eating or drinking lactose. After about age two, the body produces less lactase. Some races are more strongly affected, such as Native Americans, African-Americans, and Asians.

A common test for lactose intolerance is the hydrogen breath test. Normally, the breath contains no hydrogen. Undigested lactose is fermented by colonic bacteria to produce hydrogen, which is absorbed from the intestines, carried through the bloodstream to the lungs, and then exhaled. A child drinks a lactose-loaded beverage and is then checked for raised hydrogen levels.

Not all children need the test. A child experiencing symptoms can be taken off cow's milk and put on soy formula. If he improves, you've made the diagnosis. If you're still in doubt, talk to your doctor about a stool acidity test.

TIP

35

Caring for Teeth

Baby teeth are sturdy little creatures, but they need steady care to stay strong. From the time the first baby teeth pop through, and especially once the diet contains a wide variety of foods, they should be cleaned regularly to eliminate plaque. A cotton swab, gauze pad, or washcloth is fine at first, but by the time he can stand and walk (between twelve and fifteen months), you should get serious.

Put him on a stepstool in front of the sink and start brushing with a soft brush. The best times are after breakfast and before bed, and aim for two minutes at a brushing. Dab a small amount of toothpaste on the brush and brush in a circular motion, in front and behind the teeth. Make sure to get the bristles under the gum where bacteria hang out to eliminate plaque. Encourage him to take responsibility for brushing as soon as he develops an interest. Use reverse psychology—tell him he's just not ready yet and you *have* to do it for him!

Preventing Ear Infections

From the distant, icy shores of Finland comes a fascinating research bulletin on ear infections. Pediatricians offered more than 850 children in preschool and day care centers a syrup or chewing gum sweetened with Xylitol rather than sugar. Xylitol is known to inhibit the growth of ear infection–causing bacteria in the lab, so they tested the stuff out on kiddies. With permission, of course.

The result: The rate of ear infections was lowered by 40 percent. Good news for children prone to ear infections. You can find Xylitol gum, where it is touted as a whitener for teeth, at any drug store. If your child has had the new Prevnar vaccine, which targets the same bacteria, ear infections may go the way of chicken pox. Stay tuned for further updates.

TIP

37

Antibiotics Again?!

A major frustration parents feel over their children's health care is caused by the relentlessly runny nose, and running into the pediatrician, who is offering the third round of antibiotics in as many weeks.

Why aren't they working? Do we even *need* them? If you were a gambler, the smart money would have to be on *"no;"* you don't need them. A whole wing of the National Institutes of Health looks at "ambulatory" health care issues (that is, health issues outside hospital doors) and has consistently found, for at least the fifteen years I've been tuned in, that antibiotics are vastly overprescribed.

Most upper-respiratory infections, which include ears and sinuses, are caused by viruses that are oblivious to antibiotics. They resolve in a few days, but if you ask a busy doc if your darling son/daughter needs an antibiotic, a reflexive reach for the prescription pad gets you out a lot faster than a minilesson in biology. So if you doubt antibiotics are the right solution, don't go to the doc. Fix your child with some chicken soup instead.

TIP

38

Driving Safely?

When you think of the typical road rage aggressor, what comes to mind? Probably a male, fast food in lap, angrily extending the third finger and flooring the accelerator.

Take another look. A *Consumer Health* survey says that the soccer mom in the overjammed minivan fits the bill, too. Reasons abound: too many places to be at once; too many roadblocks; your precious, who wouldn't get dressed quickly, needed an unanticipated diaper change, or melted down at just the wrong moment . . .

If you find yourself getting angry at other drivers, hitting the brakes a bit too sharply, or using language more fit for rapper Eminem than a lady with an impressionable child in the back seat, then you're an aggressive driver. And unless you slow it down, you could hurt someone.

TIP

39

Toilet Training: Deadlines

There are any number of ways to impress upon your youngster that the day will come when he will be a proud underpants wearer. This motivation, the Promised Land of Big-Kidness, can be tied to any kind of landmark event: an upcoming trip to Disney World, the start of a new preschool year, the new baby's arrival. The best dodge I've heard was a mom telling her almost-three-year-old the store won't have any more diapers to sell in July, and that he'd have to be toilet trained by then. (The concept of July was fortunately vague enough so she could be flexible as to when July actually began.)

Toilet Training: Potty Seats

Ine of the tricks to keep up your sleeve is the incentive of purchase power. Buy a special potty seat and play it up like fireworks for the Millennium. Bring it out with a grand unveiling when she signals that she's ready to try. Playskool, Safety 1st, Right Start . . . they all make 'em. There are the self-contained potties; that is, a bowl and backing on one portable unit. Cheaper, but less versatile, is a rim that fits over the regular toilet. The advantage is that it places her on the household throne and eliminates one more transition down the road. The disadvantage is that it's not a throne just for her.

A brand-new toilet (or seat) ought to buy at least two or three genuine tries before the novelty wears off, so after the first few attempts, don't get carried away with enthusiasm for the new seat. It could backfire: If she gets it in her head that the seat is the enemy, you'll never get her on it again.

TIP

41

Kiddie Karma

The tightly wound twenty-month-old, moments away from melting down, may respond better to relaxation techniques than to talking him down. If talking isn't getting you anywhere, try these:

- Massage his back, his legs, his arms. No tickling—that will rev him up.
- Soft music—think New Age or relaxation tapes/disks rather than kiddie songs, which tend to invite interaction.
- Give him a quiet, warm snuggle or hug.
- Try ichthyotherapy: watching fish in a tank. (Thanks for this technique go to my E.R. partner Damian, who routinely recommends this to agitated patients spending too long in the waiting room.)
- Pet the pet.

TIP

42

Ready for a Bed?

Your toddler is ready for a bed somewhere between two and three years old. Long before you are, that is. Clear signs your baby is ready for a bed:

1. A loud thunk. This, along with confirmatory visual evidence, indicates T. J. or Cheyenne has just taken a header out of the crib onto the floor. The second auditory signal, a wailing cry, strongly suggests pain.
2. There are no other significant signs of readiness for a bed.

You can either transition by using a mattress on the floor or go straight to the big-boy bed. Be sure to have on hand a new set of sheets and bedding (if this is a positive, anticipated change). Alternatively, hang on to the old patterns (if sleep is traumatic enough) so the new bed resembles the old crib as much as possible.

Put up a guardrail.

Expect a lot more work as your toddler realizes how easy it is to appear in the family room with "I'm thirsty!" or "'nother story!"

TIP

43

Bad Behavior

As soon as a child becomes aware of rules, he's tempted to break them. Some broken rules are more serious than others, and that's a big lesson to learn. It starts with the word "no." Sometimes he'll test you out by violating "no" just to see how far he can go. Sometimes it stems from anger or frustration. One of the first distinctions to make in your own head is the difference between malicious behavior—pulling hair, hitting—and mischief. Mischief can be dealt with by cool, rational explanation and continued interaction.

Misbehavior born of anger or frustration requires a time-out or nap, something to separate him from the overwhelming situation he's in. If he remembers the situation later on, you can review the actions and consequences then, but don't do it in the heat of the moment.

TIP

44

Survey Says . . .

Parent-oriented magazines and Web sites periodically turn to the object of their readers' affections and ask: What do *you* want? Six-year-olds are easy: They want any and every new electronic device on the market, as well as unfettered access to them at all times. But tune in clearly to the voice of a toddler. Eliminating the static of "I want a baby sister" or "I hate my older brother," it sounds something like this:

- I don't like it when my parents yell. I love clear explanations.
- Sometimes I like new activities, but other times I like to stick to games and toys I already know.
- I can't be consistent because sometimes I'm too tired to know what I want.
- Watch me, watch me! You'd really have fun if you'd play with me too!
- I feel safe when I know the rules, even though a lot of times I like to push the edge.

TIP

45

Coping with Allergy

Any allergist will tell you—don't hold your child hostage to allergies. How to take an upbeat posture:

- Bring a safe snack to parties. Instead of ice cream, bring tofu-based ice cream.
- Alert caregivers and teachers. If a sunny day trip is planned, bring along an extra inhaler and make sure the teacher is comfortable having your child use it.
- Give your child a signal he can remember that others can learn, such as tapping his lips if he feels they're beginning to swell.
- Peanuts are everywhere and in everything. Peanut dust can get into prepared foods even if it's not a listed ingredient. Be alert.
- Carry an epinephrine pen along if for no other reason than superstitious value: If you have it you won't need it.

TIP

46

Custom Fridge Magnets

Here's an art project that will occupy an afternoon, take you through a road trip, and add a permanent, personal element to the home front.

Have him draw a family portrait—Mom, Dad, Baby Sis, the doggie(s)—and cut out each face or full-length portrait. Use crayons, paint, gouache—you pick the medium.

Next, go to your local Kinko's or other full-service copy shop; have them laminate the pictures and apply them to a firm backing. While you're out, pick up a packet of self-adhesive magnet strips from a drug store or the supermarket.

Voilá! Refrigerator magnets by your own personal *artiste en residence*.

TIP

47

Preggers Again?

Those aches and pains may not be just due to lugging around a toddler. Your body responds quickly to becoming pregnant: ligaments loosen up, blood volume increases, hormones reset their sensors in anticipation of even further adaptations down the road. You may be pregnant if you're experiencing any of the following:

- Sciatica—pain radiating down the side or back of the leg (along the pants seam); it may indicate swelling of the sciatic nerve or a loosening of the ligaments holding the backbones together.
- Carpal tunnel syndrome—pain or tingling radiating into your hand, relieved with a Velcro wrist brace.
- Leg cramps/aches—constant, burning pains in the thighs or calf muscles even in the morning, before your toddler has you running sprints.
- Heartburn, vomiting, lightheadedness— you don't need a home test when these symptoms kick in.

TIP

48

Rude Boy

"Mom, why's that lady so *FAT??*"

"I don't wanna stand next to him—he's stinky!"

Sometime around two, two and a half, a heavy dose of mortification awaits you when your precious, darling sweet pea lets loose the most atrociously thoughtless insults. Loudly.

You have to deal with the comment, but keep it in perspective. Remember that it's his way of registering wonder at the world. There's plenty he's never seen, and handicaps or distinctive physical conditions are among them. It can be difficult, frankly, not to be blown off balance by such rude statements, but it's important to respond to them. Acknowledge the differences without overreacting: "Some people are overweight, sweetie, and she may not like you to talk about it so loudly." Ignoring a comment conveys a sense of shame and extends the discomfort for the victim even more.

TIP

49

Kitchen Fun: Bread

One of the singular advances in modern life is the bread machine. Forget the personal computer or Internet—fresh bread is the greatest gift to modern man, and any child can do it:

First, toss in:
1¼ cup water
1 teaspoon sugar
1 teaspoon salt
1 tablespoon oil
1 tablespoon honey

Then add:
3 cups flour
1½ teaspoons dry yeast

Push the button and you've got challah dough. Cut it into strips and let your aspiring chef braid it just like hair.

Place the braid on a greased cookie sheet, and bake it in a preheated oven at 350°F for approximately thirty minutes. Serve it warm and fresh with jam and juice!

TIP

50

Kitchen Fun: Pizza Pie

It's never been easier to prepare your own junk food at home, another way in which today's kids have it *sooo* much better than we ever did. Moreover, you can leave the junk out!

Buy a tube of premade pizza dough and let her pound it into a round (or what passes for round) pizza crust. She can do this with minimal supervision while you chop up the tomato or grate the cheese. Spread on tomato sauce, or spritz a little olive oil if you're into pizza blanco. Get creative, or if you're not too creative, take notes from the menu next time you're at a California Pizza Kitchen. Have her prepare her favorite toppings: chicken bits, broccoli florets, pepperoni slices.

Then it's into the oven and a quick reading of *One Fish, Two Fish* until ready. *Buon appetito!*

Kitchen Fun: Cupcakes

There's the easy way to do this and there's the hard way. The hard way gets you messy: whip the batter, bake, cool, and transfer to a rack, and then on to the frosting. You know, whisking the whites, mixing and heating the sugar and corn syrup, yadda, yadda, yadda. Clean up many pots and pans.

With a hyperactive beanbag around? Nah. Go easy on yourself: cheat. The cupcake part of it isn't too hard to do from a cake mix, and after that, spread on some ready-made frosting. Then let your little Julia (or Julian) Child design it: a heart theme for Valentine's Day, green glory for St. Patty's Day, and red, white, and blue for the Fourth.

Serve 'em up when Mommy or Daddy gets home from work. These treats make a great touch for a birthday party, too.

TIP

52

Discipline Requires Discipline

The grand test of parenting a toddler is how well you manage his or her temper, just as your biggest test of parenting a baby was how well you interpret crying.

The most effective discipline tool for an out-of-control tot is your deep personal reserve of inner discipline. Limits are limits. You know what is harmful or dangerous; they don't. This is the wellspring of consistency. It takes self-discipline to say "no" to the same child in the same situation for the tenth, thirtieth, or hundredth time without giving in to irritability or annoyance.

As self-righteously satisfying as it might feel to throw out an occasional "I've already told you so a hundred times before!" it gets you nowhere in the long run. Or short run.

You have reasons to say "no," the first time or the twentieth time. End of story.

TIP

Discipline: Offer Choices

Avoid power struggles. "Because I say so" is not, by itself, reason enough for her to actually listen to you. C'mon, Mom!

While there's still time to avert a rising battle, use a diversionary tactic. Instead of telling her to pick up her toys, give her options: "Will you pick up your toys now or after you help put groceries away?" "You can eat the salad or the carrots, but I don't have anything else for a snack."

She'll have something to consider besides whether to directly confront your authority and your determination to stick to a consequence. She may choose to ignore all her choices in favor of continued misbehavior, but at least you gave it a shot.

Give yourself a little wiggle room. Ask if she would like to pick up the toys all by herself or can Mommy help? It gives her a last chance to avoid striking out, and any negotiator will tell you of the importance of a fallback position.

TIP

54

Caught in the Act— Good Girl!

The opposite of discipline, which is extinguishing bad or undesirable behavior with punishments or limitations, is lavishing praise when she does something right. We are all guilty of taking for granted small acts of daily kindness or consideration. And we all like the occasional pat on the back just for *trying* to be a nice guy. So keep your eyes and ears open for those moments when you can sing her praises: "You helped feed the baby!" "It was so nice of you to give Joshie a turn with that toy!" "I know you like playing with Fluffy and it was hard for you to give it up, but you did anyway, and Mommy is *very* proud!"

Dish out enough of these and you won't have to dish out as many punishments or time-outs.

TIP

55

Not Into Reading

Alexander loved to curl up with a good book; brother Nathan won't sit still for a moment. Several years later, you'd never be able to tell the difference between them. On some days they'll curl up with Harry Potter for an hour or more at a time, other days they're in their pirate hideaway fighting with swords and scavenging for buried treasure.

In other words, failure to read early makes not a whit of difference. It's all about language, anyway, and ample opportunities exist that don't involve books. On a drive: "That truck is blue, the next car is yellow!" Changing a diaper: "These are your knees, these are your toes!"

The issue may be attention span rather than total disinterest. A child may be willing to sit for a thirty- to sixty-second picture and game book like *Pat the Bunny*, but then he's off to another activity. Encourage language and imagination in other ways, and don't be concerned.

TIP

56

Books about Mommy and Baby

Every day and every way: It never hurts to tell a story about how much Mommy loves her bitty baby.

- *Runaway Bunny* (Margaret Wise Brown): A baby bunny plans his getaway, but his hare-brained schemes are no match for a savvy mom.
- *Owl Babies* (Martin Waddell): Three baby owls nervously await their mommy's return from the avian equivalent of Safeway. You might never remember the names in the book if, as we do, you substitute your own offspring's names instead.
- *Are You My Mother?* (P. D. Eastman): One summer, a construction crew brought some heavy equipment to our neighborhood. In the evening, we'd climb aboard the bulldozer and play a live version of the "Snort!" part of the book. Mommy would always come to the "nest" with a snack, calling it a "worm" for her little birdy.

TIP

57

Books That Celebrate Silly

Some books need no other raison d'être than their just plain old silliness.

- *Good Night, Gorilla* (Peggy Rathmann): Simian insomnia and a careless zookeeper. Available as a big, thirty-six-piece puzzle, too.
- *Wombat Stew* (Marcia K. Vaughan): An Australian gem. Complete with silly song and curious critters from Down Undah.
- *Stinky Cheese Man and Other Fairly Stupid Tales* (Jon Sciezska and Lane Smith): Explore moldy fairy tales retold with postmodern irreverence.
- *The True Story of the 3 Little Pigs* (Jon Sciezska and Lane Smith) and *The Three Little Wolves and the Big Bad Pig* (Eugene Trivizas and Helen Oxenbury): Two ways to turn the old tale on its head.

TIP

58

Book Series:
Favorite Characters

Once your toddler takes an interest in a character, the Grandma problem ("What should I bring her when I visit?") is temporarily solved.

- *Curious George:* The naughty monkey, the man in the yellow hat, the hip-hopper are all there for a new generation. Okay, maybe there have been a *few* additions.
- *Madeline:* That old house in Paris covered with vines still houses "twelve little girls in two straight lines." And poor Miss Clavel still fears a disaster!
- *Beatrix Potter:* Fat Tom Kitten pops his buttons, Peter Rabbit leaves his blue jacket behind, and the puddle ducks are still looking for their clothes. What's not to love about such critters?
- *Winnie the Pooh:* Nowadays, you have "classic" or "modern" versions. The original texts are a bit fussy and wordy, but their distinctive flavor beats the cartoony Disneyfied stuff.

TIP

59

Out-of-Control Tantrum

Sometime around month fourteen or fifteen you and meteorologists will know the phenomenon: A little squall unexpectedly turns into a raging nor'easter. The same uncooperative toy (or Daddy's shoe) that he's been batting around contentedly all afternoon is suddenly flung across the staircase banister. He knocks his head against the wall, starts wailing, and throwing everything in sight. Nothing, and I mean *nothing*, will chill him out. Any help you offer is met with rising fury and flailing limbs.

All storms pass, even the big ones. Sure, they leave damage and destruction in their wake, but they all end. When your little guy's tempest has reached hurricane proportions, batten down the hatches. Make sure he can't hurt himself or irreparably destroy valuables and ride it out. Swaddle him exactly as you did when he was a baby. Once the winds subside, he'll feel much better, and the sun will come out again.

TIP

60

Meltdown Madness

True nuclear meltdowns are often attributed to an easily identifiable cause: fatigue. His batteries need a recharge and he's not ready to take a nap. I daresay that many a meltdown is triggered by the mere mention of naptime.

When possible, trick him. If an afternoon playtime that immediately precedes a nap is becoming the setup for a knock-down, drag-out tantrum, change the scene, Gene. Give him a bath, offer a snack, read a book quietly (no bouncing and sound effects while reading) before you lay him down for his snooze.

Toddlers develop emotions before they develop the tools to deal with them; cranky weariness is something he'll share with you in its pure, unadulterated form.

TIP

61

Add Ten Minutes

As a baby, your child was docile, passive, and went wherever you went whenever you wanted. She got hungry or needed a change at inconvenient times, but essentially, she was a passenger. The times, they are a-changin'. Now, she's making up her own mind about the clothes she wants to wear; whether she watches a video until the end; and how fast, or slow, she wants to eat her food. It's the control thing. She wants a share of the decision making, no matter how little she comprehends the art.

The easy way to finesse this is always to allow an extra ten minutes at both ends of whatever errand or job it is you need to do. Give her a heads up: "We're going to leave in five minutes," but give it with ten minutes' lead-time. She will throw a hissy fit unless things are just right and, as you well know, things are *never* just right.

Art Project:
Popsicle-Stick Family

Popsicle sticks. Yes, Popsicle sticks. Skinny ones, fat ones. Short ones, tall ones. Just like people.

Hey! Wait a second! There's an idea! Turn Popsicle sticks into people! Have him draw faces, one for each family member. Then glue a few more together to make the body. Alternatively, cut outfits out of construction paper and glue them on a backbone stick. Once your little Dr. Frankenstein has completed the whole family, stick the whole gang into a planter and paint the family name on it.

Be sure to include any pets. They have feelings, too, you know.

TIP

63

Art Project: Percussion Section

For families with a supernaturally high noise tolerance, make a home percussion orchestra. Any inverted tub, pot, or food container is an instant drum. Make a shaker from any container filled with uncooked pasta, nuts, or beans. A tambourine is whipped up by stapling together two paper plates with dried beans in between. Cymbals? You have pot covers, don't you?

Get a couple of his friends together on a play date, and throw a cassette into the tape player. Then have them play along with their songs.

How do you think Pearl Jam got started?

TIP

64

Art Project: Play Dough

There is, of course, no reason in the world why you should ever have to cook up your own play dough. Except it can be good ol' messy fun. The recipe:

3 cups flour
1½ cups salt
6 teaspoons cream of tartar
3 cups water
⅓ cup cooking oil
Food coloring

Toss the dry ingredients in a bowl, blend the oil, water, and tartar together in another bowl. Add the wet stuff to the dry stuff. Mix well. Cook the resultant muck on a low heat until rubbery. Then let it cool and knead slightly. Put her down for a nap as it's cooling. If this isn't a bargaining chip to get her to take a nap, I don't know what is.

TIP

Toilet Training: Juicy Poops

About the time you're ready for the back-and-forth of toilet training, you might find yourself blind-sided by the disgusting phenomenon of juicy poops.

These are massive, sloppy, slimy bowel movements resulting from an exclusive diet of fruit juice. Sure, a juice box or cup is more nutritious than chips, but the stealthy, constant refills rob your toddler of a normal mealtime.

The torrent of sweets descending through his intestines are more than his body needs, so the sugar never gets absorbed by his intestines. Eventually they land in the large intestine, accompanied by a significant water load. This is physiology: all those extra glucose and sucrose molecules are "balanced" by a water molecule. Ipso facto, presto change-o: diarrhea.

So before you can step forward and step out of diapers, take a step back. Cut down on the juice until his movements are firm enough to give potty the old toddler try.

TIP

66

Toilet Training: Aim Games

Find a biodegradable object that can safely ride the plumbing (cereal is ideal) and toss a small handful in the bowl. Get ready, get set . . . take aim! Pick out an individual corn flake (or bread ball) to flip or sink, and voila! One dry toddler.

Boys, naturally, have a better advantage than girls playing this game (a situation unlikely to occur for the remainder of their natural lifetimes), but with a little imagination it can work for girls, too. Wait until a cluster of corn flakes are underneath her, and then have her pee on them as far away as she can. Where there's a will—and a full bladder—there's a way.

TIP

67

Toilet Training: Books That Help

Every conceivable insight into the toileting process has made it into print, designed exclusively for the eyes of kids.

- *Flush the Potty!* (Wilson-Max) employs the gimmicky trick of providing a button that makes an electronic flush to while away hours sitting on the pot.
- In the tabloid, confessional genre, *"Uh Oh! Gotta Go!"* (McGrath and Dieterichs) shares other toddlers' experiences trying, trying, trying.
- A pop-up book, *What Do You Do with a Potty?* (Borgardt and Chambliss) is for the more visually oriented.
- The favorite in our house, however, was *Everyone Poops* (Gomi & Stinchecum). This prized tome lays it all out: a multitude of animal poos lovingly illustrated, even some portrayed in the act itself. I'm not sure how this actually helps internalize the struggle to relinquish waste, but it sure captures the imagination.

TIP

- Last is *Once Upon a Potty* (Frankel). There are two versions—Joshua for boys; Prudence for girls. This popular book tells the age-old story of refusal and then surrender to the bowl.

Mommy's Not Supposed to Get Sick!

The darkest moment of any toddler's life is to catch Mom or Dad in a vulnerable moment: Mommies are not supposed to get sick. The reality is that from the time the first slice of turkey falls onto the platter at Thanksgiving until a mug of green beer is downed on St. Patty's Day, it's one cold or flu bug after another. At some point you're going to come down with something yourself.

This is when the essential unfairness of parenting really shines through. You wake up feeling like a meat hammer has been working you over all night, sinuses and nasal passages are filled with sludge. The first thing you'll want to do is head back to bed ASAP, but no such luck.

Drag yourself through feeding him breakfast; then park him in front of a video. Don't be surprised if he's not interested and gets clingy when he sees how crummy you feel. He'll want to climb in bed with you, cry and carry on just for some attention—which you're incapable of providing. This is when he gets a big assignment: Tell him that he's your doctor and has to give you medicine to feel better. Watch him rise to the occasion.

TIP

69

Lemme Help!

A ny self-respecting two-year-old wants to
help. They want to make that transition
from being a handful to being helpful.
(Inconsistently, yes, but the sprouting seedlings
of a helpmate are there.) It makes him feel all
grown up. Take the opportunity of turning it
into a learning experience. Some suggestions:

- Sort the laundry (emphasizes color
  learning).
- Pick up his toys by size and types
  (have different baskets available).
- Water the plants (preferably outside).
- Sort silverware from the dishwasher.
- Put away groceries.

TIP

70

Scary Monsters

How do you enter the mind of an eighteen-month-old? Play along with their games. When she's playing animals and roars like a lion, recoil in fear, saying, "I'm so scared of big lion!" She'll be delighted at how fearsome she is. Repeat this two or three times, and then roar back, since now you're the big lion.

As she switches from animal to animal, you'll get an insider's view of how she understands the similarities and differences between the creatures she's encountered. Watch how she imitates a cat's snuggling/purring behavior, or a dog's yapping. It's a good way to teach her that when a cat arches its back or a dog growls, it's a signal to leave them alone.

And by letting her pace the game, you'll get a sense of how long (or short) her attention span is, even for activities she really likes.

TIP

71

The Box the Big TV Comes In

A fabulously durable plaything is the big box that comes with a new TV. In our house, it has made a great clubhouse, but it has also served as a puppet theater, a planetarium, a subway, a fortress, an art gallery, and a platform. The last choice is one to be avoided, especially for those of you with sofa-jumpers.

I recommend the judicious use of "If you do that one more time I'm going to take it away" threats, however. Since it is such a versatile toy, you really don't want to get rid of a TV box until you absolutely have to.

Mail Call

A something-from-nothing trick is to turn a shoebox into your child's very own mailbox. Decorate it yourself, or have her make her own drawings; teach her the letters of her name; cut out a door for the mail. Use a paper hinge on a Popsicle-stick flag to announce when the mail's in.

Since kids love mail, let her handle all the junk mail and catalogs. Every now and then, put in a special Someone Luvs You card. Have Grandma and Grandpa send a special note for her box. She'll have the kind of relationship with the mail that we can all be jealous of: no bills, no warning notices, no credit card solicitations.

Bedtime Trick: Good-Night Toys!

For those with the just-getting-her-to-bed-is-a-chore issues, enlist the aid of her best friends Jujube and Mrs. Winnipissaukee. Ask your daughter to be the mommy and put her toys and dolls to sleep.

Give her a little bit of room and see what you can learn. You may discover that she doesn't like to read a story before putting her "babies" to bed. Or, she may offer a glass of water or sing a song.

Fine-tune her bedtime ritual to match what she's doing and she just might be a little more willing to go along with you.

TIP

74

Body Mass Index

Do you need to go on that diet? Maybe just exercise more? Sure, both would help. Sure, boneheaded advice like this is as enlightening as telling you not to stick your baby's head into a bowl full of piranhas.

There is, however, a nice, scientifically sound way to objectify a sensationally touchy subject. The body mass index, or BMI, corresponds to an optimal weight. Too high a BMI means you're overweight, and at higher risk for heart disease, hypertension, and diabetes. The exact formula follows.

(Weight in pounds) ÷ (Height in inches)^2 × 705 = BMI

You can find this on any parenting or health site on the Net, along with advice on what to do if you don't like the number. The ideal index range is 21–24. These sites won't tell you how to balance the "have tos" of a two-year-old against the "ought tos" of regular exercise—you have to figure that one out on your own.

And note this: The BMI calculator doesn't work for athletes, body builders, or frail elderly folk. It also should be thrown out for pregnant or nursing women.

TIP

75

More Diet Math

Serious about losing the weight this time? Good! Let's run some more numbers for you. To tell how many calories you need to stay the same weight:

- [Weight (lb.) × 15] = calories per day you need to maintain your weight if you have an active lifestyle.
- Multiply weight by 13 calories per day for a sedentary lifestyle (may not apply to mothers of toddlers).
- To allow for weight loss, multiply the number above by 0.7.

For example: Let's say you're 130 pounds. That's 1,950 calories per day to stay at this weight, or 1,690 for those of you who plop down in front of the computer each day and don't get up until dinnertime. (Like certain baby-book authors I could mention . . .) To lose weight, that drops to 1,365 calories per day, or a mere 1,183 for you more sedentary types.

On this tight caloric budget, be sure to start a food diary, and offer yourself rewards (no, not food) just like you would for your well-behaving, good-listening two-and-a-half-year-old.

TIP

76

Don't Nag Me, Mommy!

The most dreaded self-revelatory moment is to hear yourself sounding like your parents. Casual eavesdropping in play groups reveals that the most intense bonding arises from sharing hideous mommy tales. And the top sayings guaranteed to make you cringe in horror are:

- "When I was your age . . ."
- "I've told you [*insert number, arbitrarily large*] times already!"
- "You never/always [*undesirable behavior here*]!"
- "Enough TV!"

Try these non-nag versions instead:

- "That's unacceptable behavior."
- "Now we'll have to put [*x*] away. I'm sorry, you had your chance."
- "Mommy doesn't want you to get hurt."

Down the road, many years from now, when she's taking your darling, perfect grandchild to her play group, she'll also sound like her parents—only a better version.

TIP

77

Toddler Traffic Signs

The following advice involves buying lumber and a street sign, but it's potentially a lifesaver. Make a traffic sign and place it in the middle of the street:

STOP!
[Toddler's name]
At Play!

Especially for those living on a cul-de-sac, it will slow down inconsiderate teenage (or older) drivers, who don't quite *get it*.

TIP

78

"No" Means "I Don't Know!"

"Wanna go to the park?"

"No!"

"But you love the park!"

"NO!"

"Okay, we'll stay here and play."

"NO NO NO!"

Been there? Done that? If so, you may have discovered that "no" doesn't automatically mean "no." It means "I'm going to be in charge for a little bit, now." Sometimes, offering a couple of choices gets to yes: "We can go to the park or we can go to the playground." "Wan' park!" (Yes, I know that a park is a playground, but *he* thinks he's getting a choice!)

And sometimes the best no-buster is to make a game of it: "Every time you say 'no,' I'm going to give you a kiss." This won't get you anywhere any faster, but you're sure to enjoy your day a whole lot more.

TIP

79

"No" Means "No!"

Even if his "no" doesn't really mean "no," occasionally he ought to get away with being boss. If he's not hungry at lunch or dinnertime, he'll be hungry sooner or later. If he wants to walk instead of being pushed in the stroller, so be it. Let him push the stroller, and in a few minutes he'll crawl back in.

Up the ante: Does he want to drink from a big-kid, that is, lidless, glass? Risk the spill. Let him understand this indulgence is only permissible in a limited, low-maintenance area like the kitchen. (And then don't gripe about cleaning up if you so indulged him!)

He doesn't want the clothes you've picked? You go, boy. Let him pick, but remind him that there's a chance he may miss the movie you were planning to see if he takes too long.

TIP

80

Ten Different Ways to Say No

Oh, how the sound of "no" wears after a while. Day in, day out: "If I told you once, I told you a hundred times!" Puh *leez*. Spare yourself the misery of becoming a harpy. Try these:

1. "Only if you eat your cereal first."
2. "If you like it so much, we'll play with it later when I can watch and make sure it doesn't break."
3. "Go ahead, half pint, make my day!"
4. "Hot! *HOT!*"
5. "Remember the rock? What happened at the playground? That's when we learned what 'hurt' means!"
6. "That'll be so much more fun for you after you've rested." Note judicious avoidance of *n* word (nap) here.
7. "If you do that, Barney says good-bye forever!"
8. "The president called and said *he* wanted to play with it now."
9. "The doggie's already licked it, so it may have some bad germs on it."
10. "Yes." (This only works on no-means-yes and yes-means-no day.)

Now make up some of your own . . .

TIP

81

Toilet Paper Conservation

The author T. Coraghessan Boyle wrote in *A Friend of the Earth:* "To be a friend of the earth, you have to be an enemy of the people." Nothing quite tears at our buried eco-consciousness (interred underneath years' worth of disposable-diaper landfill) like the sight of a toddler mesmerized by the unwinding toilet paper roll.

There are ways to thwart his manic wastefulness. Put a rubber band around the roll, crimp the inner cardboard to slow the unraveling, place the roll on an upper shelf.

But the surest way to avoid this wholly unnecessary waste is to forgo toilet paper altogether until he's a little older. Use a tissue box instead. Even if he develops a fascination with pulling out tissues one by one, it's still a lot slower than a whizzing roll of Mr. Whipple's best.

TIP

Kitchen Fun:
Ice-Cream Potato

On a snowy evening in Colorado, in a warm inn after a hard day conquering the slopes, we came across a dessert that has become the family favorite, an ice cream potato. Our thanks to the waitress who invented it and shared her recipe:

1. Scoop out some hard vanilla ice cream and mold it into the shape of a potato.
2. Roll the potato in cocoa; then cover it with chocolate sprinkles.
3. Slice open lengthwise and spritz on whipped cream. Voilá! Ice-cream potato!

TIP

83

Kitchen Fun: Sloppy Joes

On a co-o-o-o-old December day, a weekend, say, when Dad's home, turn lunch into an activity. A Sloppy Joe sandwich is basically thick meat sauce on a bun, and the easiest thing in the world to make, even for a two-year-old.

1. Toss an onion and celery stalk into the chopper. Let him push all the buttons in whatever order he likes.
2. Daddy's job: brown the onion and celery mix with ground beef in a skillet.
3. Drain the oil; then stir in tomato sauce, Worcestershire sauce, ketchup, and whatever other ingredients you desire.
4. Set the table while it thickens up.
5. Serve on a toasted bun.

Rename the concoction a Sloppy Sally or Sloppy Sammy. (Who was Joe, anyway?)

TIP

84

When to Stay Home from Day Care: Illnesses

There are a few simple, commonsense reasons for day care to be out of the question. Pushing emotions firmly aside (I *can't* take off from work one more day!), you don't want to expose other children to whatever your girl has—never mind the fact that she picked it up from a day care friend. She's going to be miserable and clingy; there's just no use fighting it. Keep her home.

The symptoms indicating she's contagious and capable of spreading germs are:

- Fever over 100.4° F
- Vomiting and/or diarrhea
- A generalized rash (except for poison ivy)
- Moist cough (a dry asthmatic cough need not be quarantined)
- A "barky" or "croupy" cough
- Mouth sores
- Pink eye

TIP

85

When to Stay Home from Day Care: Injuries

Far less clear-cut than keeping a sick child home is whether to keep a child home after an injury. The generalizations are trickier, since individual circumstances vary tremendously:

- If he needs repeated pain medication for a broken bone, or a serious sprain, within the last two to three days
- The first twenty-four to thirty-six hours of having a cut stitched, to prevent reinjuring the same area
- Limping

Things that do not confine a child to home:

- A cast or splint that does not interfere with "normal" toddler activities
- Stitches older than twenty-four to thirty-six hours that can be covered by a small bandage
- Minor bruises
- Minor head injuries (the child acts and eats normally)

TIP

86

Making Sense of: Antihistamines

When managing a cold at home, deciphering the shelves upon shelves of cold remedies seems like a daunting task. In truth, it couldn't be easier: nothing works, so don't even bother. Still not convinced? All right, here's the primer.

Two main ingredients, antihistamines and decongestants, are the backbone of all cold medications. It's worth getting to know them.

Antihistamines inhibit production of mucus in the respiratory tract. The histamine signal that causes congestion is blocked by the drug. You can tell if a medication is an antihistamine because it usually ends in –*amine* (brompheniramine, diphenhydramine, chlorpheniramine).

The reason they don't work is because the mucous blockade varies greatly, and at best antihistamines do only a modest job. More reliably, they make your child sleepy, which may be a good or bad thing, depending on how awful a day you each are having.

Making Sense of: Decongestants

Decongestants, in contrast to antihistamines, constrict blood vessels along the respiratory tract and thereby shrink the swollen tissues. They are a little more reliable than antihistamines, but with far more side effects, which are more obnoxious as well. They can cause irritability, insomnia, rapid heartbeat and tremor, even nausea and vomiting.

There are three common decongestants available: phenylpropanolamine (gotcha! not an antihistamine), pseudoephedrine, and phenylephrine. (Think P words.) The reason decongestants work well with antihistamines is that the insomnia/wakefulness balances out the sedation. In theory, anyway. In actual practice, they produce a sleepy and irritable tyke with dried-out, crusty ruts in his nose that can only be sandblasted away.

One last caveat for both medications: The body adapts to these extra chemicals within two or three days. It overproduces histamine and blocks the blood vessel shrinkage. This means that the recommended doses are no longer adequate. Don't give more; give up. The cold will be gone in a day or two anyway.

TIP

88

Children's Food Pyramid

The USDA adapted its food pyramid for the needs of two- to six-year-olds because one size didn't fit all tastes. USDA nutritionists survey national food consumption to identify foods that kids this age actually eat. They compared actual choices to known nutritional needs—and found that kids were, more or less, already eating what they needed. So the pyramid should help parents fine-tune what their children are already choosing for themselves. The main difference between grownups and kids, to the USDA, is that kids need more fat. It helps grow the body's machinery—contrary to adults, in whom excess fat only serves to decay the structures.

Other points the pyramid aims for are minor nudges rather than full-scale roadblocks. For instance, rather than juice, which is mostly sugar, whole fruits containing more fiber, minerals, and vitamins are recommended. Potatoes and tomatoes are popular choices, but are suggested as a baked potato or salad, rather than as fries or sauce, which contain excess salt, fat, and sugar.

You can find more information on the Web at *www.usda.gov/cnpp/KidsPyra*.

TIP

89

Klutz Books

Klutz books are complete entertainment packs ideal for back-seat travel or for sitting around waiting for a grown-up appointment to finish. Available are:

- Drawing, sticker, and painting books
- Board game and magic books
- Kids cooking and science/experiment books (and after all, what is cooking but a little experimenting with food textures and tastes?)
- Kids' travel books, complete with back-seat games, mazes, puzzles, and Benadryl

(Well, okay, maybe not the Benadryl.)

Discipline Doubts

No report card comes at the end of the term; no parent-teacher conference is scheduled to review your strengths or where you have room to improve. Fact is, you're going to have to wait until he's raising his own kids to really see if you did right by your child.

Every night, going to bed, it's normal to reflect on how consistent you've been. If you've been just indulgent enough, yet meted out punishments firmly and fairly. You might wonder if he still loves you.

Share this with your partner, with the other parents in your neighborhood, or online. Measure each other's doubts against your own and gauge the household—or community— norms. You need to have an understanding between you as parents to support each other and avoid showing your toddler your inconsistencies.

TIP

91

Discipline: Natural Consequences

Not every oppositional act requires a directing, controlling response from a parent. Some misdeeds have their own natural consequences. Throwing a toy into the fireplace and breaking it closes the matter. No more toy. He'll have to choose one from the mountain of other toys available. Tearing up a favorite book means you cannot read it anymore—and you won't get a new one. Spilling juice out of the cup, after being repeatedly told not to, means there's none left. If he's thirsty, he'll have to drink water.

Naturally, withholding a meal in order to make a point is going too far. Remind him when he asks for the book or toy again. He won't begin to internalize that his actions led to specific consequences until he actually feels them for himself. It might take a long time, but one day he'll start to be a little more careful.

TIP

92

Discipline: Respect Feelings

"We didn't have complexes in my day," says my mom. Sure. They had cows to shoe and horses to milk. Or whatever. But the black-and-white world of years past is gone, and in our Technicolor times, a better way is possible.

Don't use words that hurt when tamping down a temper. Respect his feelings even when your own are raging in the red zone. Indulging in anger may feel like an easy solution when you're not being listened to, but it has repercussions. He'll feel shame and guilt; so will you. Children push you to the limit because they want to see what happens. It gets personal, since you're the dad or mom, but they don't know how to control themselves any better. They're still trying to get it right.

Discipline: Never Spank

If you think words hurt, just wait till you see what a slap can do. Never, *ever, ever* hurt a child because they're misbehaving or not listening. It teaches that violence and an abuse of superior strength is sometimes okay. Children who are hit cower in fear and still don't understand any better. It stops them from doing the misbehavior, and it does so faster than most other methods. But all they learn is that some deeds earn them pain and that it may be okay for them to inflict pain, too.

I know, of course, that few parents resort to spanking anymore. And I know that few would accept other parents disciplining children in this way. But the impulse is human, even if you never indulge it, so it's always helpful to have tools, and reasons, to talk yourself out of these dark impulses when they do surface.

TIP

94

Stuff

Acouple of years ago, I came across a small
independent band called The Want, whose
CD was called *Too Much Stuff*. I gave it a second
look mostly because it was how I was feeling
about our household after our second son's first
birthday and right before the Midwinter
Holiday 'n' Gift Extravaganza. (You know
which one I'm talking about.)

After even a year, *stuff* really piles up: toys,
clothes, paraphernalia. With the second baby, it
accumulates exponentially. The toy pieces get
smaller; the quantity is boundless.

Plan ahead for a storage area for your
toddler; invest in organizers; have a clear color-
and name-coded labeling system; and, above all,
put toys back together at the end of each day.
Nothing makes a toddler more disinterested in
toys than missing parts. They'll move on to the
next toy rather than search for the pieces they
scattered to the winds (or the gap behind the
couch) a day ago.

Un-Stuffing

A good way to alleviate some of the guilty too-much-stuff blues is to periodically give some away. Especially at the holiday season (though no need to wait for winter, either), take stock of your child's *least* favorite toys. Don't solicit his advice, he'll tell you *every* one is still his favorite. He'll put on an exaggerated show playing with them to prove it. He won't let you take away a single one of them.

Remove them on your own. Hospitals, especially children's hospitals, gladly accept clean, working toys. They don't accept stuffed animals, however, because of infection and allergy considerations. These institutions generally serve an indigent population, so the toys are always welcome.

Homeless shelters are also a worthy site for toy donation, and they *will* accept stuffed animals. Don't donate broken toys, ragged stuffed animals, or toys with missing pieces. It's not charity to give away something that properly belongs in the trash.

TIP

96

No Go

You know the sound, the gr-r-r-unt. You may be more used to hearing it come from your Uncle Maury, but your little guy can get constipated all too easily, too. Children who wait three or more days to poop have a problem: the longer a stool remains in the colon, the more it hardens. This is because the physiological function of the large intestine is to remove water from digested food.

A diet that's big on bread, cupcakes, and burgers is skinny on fiber. So to prevent constipation, up the fiber-rich foods in his daily diet. Consider the apple. Consider apricots. Whole-grain bread. Fiber-fortified muffins or cookies. None of these are as sweet as, say, Chucky Pickles's Chocomania Cookie Bits'n'Sugar, but an unlimited diet of such foodstuffs is not good, either. Remember one of the basics of feeding a child: he'll eat what's in front of him.

The other remedy is to increase the amount of water in his diet or, in a crisis, high-sugar fruit juice such as apple or grape juice. Don't start on enemas (yeah, kids need them occasionally) or suppositories until checking with your doc first.

TIP

97

Sun Block Spray

When you were a teen, a beach trip was simple: toss a bikini, shorts, tank top, underwear, Coppertone, and shades into a bag the size of a toothbrush holder, and *vrooom!* "Hello, Jersey!"

Now, with the stroller, the sun-tent, the cooler, the toys . . . and the Humvee to haul them all sunward, it takes about a day just to adequately mobilize. Gone are the hazy days of yore, but whatcha gonna do?

One smart thing we do now is to apply the sun block *before* going out. Here's why: Sun block is a chemical that filters out both UV-B (which cause burns) and UV-A rays (which are thought to cause skin aging). The chemical protection works after twenty to thirty minutes of bonding with skin cells. The time to apply it is *before* you're out in the sun. It only works if the skin isn't wet, another reason to lather up before hitting the waves. Your child's skin can fry in the twenty minutes before it starts to work.

TIP

Spray-block comes in all SPFs and may even take less holding-still time. Ideal for squirmy, squiggly types, and when you've got more than one kid to do.

98

Sun Block Stay!

A fter twelve or so minutes of baking under the sun, the waves begin to look more and more appealing. Even to the most timid of tots. After you've had a hearty round of splish-splashing around in the surf, it'll be snack and juice time (rehydrate, rehydrate, rehydrate!), but it's also time to reapply and reapply. There is no such thing as a waterproof sun block, therefore "water-resistant" or "all-day protection" claims are pure bunko. And there's definitely no such thing as a towel-proof sun block.

If your sunny-day foray is into the hills instead of the beach, look for bug repellent, too—Avon's Skin-so-Soft, for example. This is a flea/tick/mosquito repellent that'll keep your children comfortable and offer protection against cooties such as Lyme disease and others you may never have heard of—like ehrlichiosis or babesiosis. Trust me: they're out there, too.

Last, but not least: remember the high-UV hours are 11 A.M. to 3 P.M. Avoid direct sunlight during those hours: it goes a long way to limiting long-term skin toxicity—like cancer.

TIP

Toothbrush Strike

The time to begin caring for teeth is when they appear. No *problemo*. Until, that is, labor and management butt heads, and it's time to strike. A predictable test of wills. Strike negotiation tactics:

- Rewards: A sticker for a good brushing job, trade in five or ten stickers for even better rewards.
- A selection of brushes: Rugrats, Barbie, Arthur, Blues Clues. He picks the friend to brush with.
- Tag team I: He starts; you finish. No reward unless you get to "help."
- Tag team II: Let him do your teeth (with your brush, of course); then you do his.
- "Dentist *said* you have to! Otherwise your teeth will get sick."
- Don't take no for an answer. If none of the above succeed in changing his mind, let him throw a tantrum, give a time-out, but at the end of it, make it clear that he's got to get his teeth brushed. This is *not* negotiable.

TIP

100

Chalk Talk

A game that became a neighborhood favorite was tracing our daughter's outline on the driveway, then drawing a playground around her—slide, swings, tree, sunny sky. Pretty soon all the kids wanted to play in the playground, and everybody got to decorate their own outline.

The rain that washed it all away was actually welcome, since it let us start all over again.

Not recommended for families of homicide detectives.

Alternative Asthma Remedies 1

Caveat emptor: The benefits of herbal medications are in exact proportion to the dangers. Herbs in their natural state are a source of hundreds of chemicals and compounds, of which the desired drug is but one. The amount of healing, therapeutic drugs in herbs in their raw state varies greatly from plant to plant, root to root, and even leaf to leaf.

Ephedrine is used by asthmatics and dieters; it's also known as ephedra or Ma Huang. It is a stimulant that dilates constricted bronchi but also raises blood pressure, increases heart rate, and, if you give an uncontrolled amount, can cause stroke, psychosis, and death.

The FDA recommends a max of 8 milligrams a serving of herbal ephedrine for adults—appropriate kiddie doses are not even mentioned—and for no more than seven days. Because of the inherent natural variability in strength and concentration, some supplements have been found to contain over 100 milligrams per serving.

My recommendation: Don't try any of these products on your toddler.

Alternative Asthma Remedies 2

The number of herbal asthma products competing against traditional medications can make your head spin. These products claim alternative, magical cures based on a heritage traced back to antiquity. What they don't tell you is that all these old, dead folks might say, "It didn't really help much."

Part of the appeal lies in the very antiscientific origin. Most folks forget that plants' array of chemicals and poisons are designed for the sheer purpose of defeating their own natural enemies. Hemlock is as natural as caffeine, but I don't recommend it for asthmatics.

Among the herbs touted to cure asthma are eucalyptus, saw palmetto, bayberry, ginkgo, *Zizyphus spinosa* (jujube), peppermint, and wild cherry bark. None are proven and none are likely to hurt your child in *small* amounts—unless you forsake other medications that are proven to work.

Go to the American Academy of Allergy, Asthma and Immunology (*www.aaaai.org*) for clear, useful, unbiased help.

TIP

103

The Art of Listening

The deceptively easy job of listening to your toddler can prove to be a most daunting task. It involves shifting your focus away from each of a hundred other distractions: the phone, e-mail, Rosie.

You hear the cute stuff when you listen: what fascinated her, what song she learned, what matters to her. When you're distracted, you *miss* the important stuff: the budding vocabulary, the baby steps toward figuring out the whole, huge world around her.

Even if all she wants to do is tell you that doggie made a poo in the park, she's providing ground-level skinny from the perspective of a two-year-old. By gracing her with your undivided attention, you also reinforce that her unique perspective is respected and important to someone else. That's what empowerment is all about, right? See how young it starts? And that's why the simple tasks are the biggest ones: because so much rides on them.

TIP

104

Consistency Counts

Consistency counts. Every discipline and guidance rule you lay down is tested hour by hour, day by day. So the task laid out for *you* is every bit as challenging as the one you set for your child.

This is an uphill battle. Your mood varies from one day to the next, and circumstances on a happy Tuesday morning are different than on a hectic Friday evening. That's why, when the heating bill *triples* and your husband calls in telling you not to hold dinner up for him—the same day, of course, that Mom called to ask if a three-week visit starting next week is okay—*that's* why he chooses that moment to push baby's bouncy seat and dump the cake batter all over the kitchen floor. He just wants to test out if you really meant it when you said, "Be careful with baby."

Don't indulge in the impulse to rage or scream. He gets a time-out and no more, no less. Conversely, in the flush of a raise, a big sale for your company, or news that your brother is finally getting married, don't let him tear toys away from baby. Consistency may be the hobgoblin of small minds, but it's the foundation of good behavior.

TIP

105

Rules for Rule Bending

Bending the rules is a great challenge—because you have to explain the exception to a two-year-old. Changing the rules is not the same as being too tired or too busy or too excited to enforce the rules.

There will be moments when he's behaved especially well all day, or he's at a special celebration where allowances can be made so the good times can last. If you're letting him stay up late, preface it with: "Tonight is special. It's Thanksgiving dinner and we have company, so you can stay up with us." Or: "We don't always have cake for dessert, but today is Zoe's birthday, so we're having a treat."

Modifying a rule for a special circumstance teaches flexibility and encourages problem-solving skills. And no one is gonna hold it against you.

TIP

106

P.S. Drop Off *All* the Kids

The following cautionary tale is from the Don't-let-this-happen-to-you archives. Our local paper ran a story in the Metro section back in 1999 about a guy, could have been any guy, who forgot something.

His mornings were crazy, the story ran. He got the kids up and ready for their day, piled them into the van, parceled them out to three destinations and then went to work. A juggling act familiar to all.

One day, it all fell apart. Amid the everyday chaos, according to the story, he forgot he had his twenty-month-old daughter in the back of the van. The toddler was discovered crying but unharmed five and a half hours later by a passerby, who called police. The daddy was mortified. He had been distracted, he confessed, and thought he had dropped her off! She had been sound asleep, and her car seat was directly behind the driver's seat, out of his line of sight.

His wife was sympathetic. She understood completely what had happened and said it could have happened to her, too. Precisely. So do not just trust a glance in the rearview.

TIP

107

Earplugs

The best name in earplugs is Mack's, and they are now available in child sizes. They're not just for swimming, bathing, or showering. If a noise-sensitive two-year-old can't take the colicky crying of his baby sister (especially when he's trying to go to sleep), he may accept the trade-off of the funny sensation of earplugs in exchange for a little peace and quiet.

On a plane trip, these block the sensitive eardrum from all painful pressure changes. They're made of silicone, which expand in the heat of a 98.6° ear and make for a comfortable, yet tight, seal.

Doesn't Like Table Food?

In a recent *Contemporary Pediatrics* magazine for pediatricians, I came across the following dilemma: a two-year-old's mom worried that her son only ate stage-two or stage-three baby food. No table food. The doc's responses were reasoned and thorough:

- Do a developmental check: If gross and fine motor skills are okay and there has been no difficulty in chewing or swallowing in the past (both complicated ballets of muscle coordination), then it's not a developmental problem.
- Do a nutrition check: A balanced diet is a balanced diet. Form is less important than overall intake of proper nutrients.
- Check oral health: The child in the article had late-erupting teeth, but was otherwise normal. Cavities or gingivitis might be a factor.
- Evaluate temperament, behavior: Absent any of the above problems, this may just be testing or oppositional behavior.

Rx: 99 percent of the time you can just let the fad play itself out.

TIP

109

Fast-Food Toys

News flash: You get what you pay for. Each year, just in time for Christmas, the Consumer Product Safety Commission releases their dirty-dozen list of the most dangerous toys available to kids. Almost always at the top (or occupying several choice spots on the list) are fast-food chain giveaways. A consistent problem is that these small toys are choking hazards, in whole or in part—from the pieces that break off easily (shoddy workmanship, don't you know).

Don't McDonald's, Wendy's, and Burger King get it? Kids *already* have too many toys. Do they really need the movie tie-in to keep families marching through the door? Do they think we're idiots? We'll always sacrifice nutrition for convenience. We don't need a cheap, plastic, instantly forgettable toy to lure us in.

TIP

110

Timmy the Biter

W hat do you do with a biter? It's a common, albeit unacceptable, habit and has little to do with a child's temperament. It may be more of a developmental issue: A child who bites in the social setting of a play group or day care may not have other social or language skills to resolve tense feelings. For instance, when Sammy grabs the ball, Timmy bites back because he can't ask for it back without a lot of frustration.

Circumstances may also conspire against him. A new baby who nurses all the time is "biting" mommy, so big brother may decide that's the best way to grab the limelight.

Because the consequences are serious, solutions need to be serious as well. Removing Timmy from the play group until the habit has been abandoned is one way; a short course in behavior modification by a psychologist may be another.

TIP

Playground Alert

Some playgrounds have hidden hazards, so here are ways to make sure it's safe:

- On the ground, dirt, wood chips, and rubber are the best surfaces to land on. They *give* on impact, from a little to a lot, and that can prevent a trip to the ER complete with CAT scan.
- Climbing equipment should be no more than six feet off the ground.
- Swings should be spaced far enough apart so children don't collide.
- Inspect chains and flat surfaces for rust, deterioration, or broken parts.

Public parks are under supervision of local or county recreation authorities. Look for a sign with a phone number or Web site to register complaints or dangers. E-mail won't do the job—talk to a human being who has children, nieces, or cousins of his own who might have a personal interest in fixing the problem.

TIP

112

Dress Barn

The daily process of dressing yourself only becomes a seamless activity—if you're lucky—sometime in the second or third year of marriage. Think about it: As a high school or college student, the choice of what to put on made a blaring statement about who you were. You didn't consider it a light matter. And dressing for work, or to attract a spouse? C'mon—it's a big issue!

Why be surprised, then, if the act of getting dressed is important to a toddler? Why question the fact that the bedroom turns into a barnyard of scattered clothes, socks, and underpants just to put on the same sweats and T-shirt she wore yesterday?

Dressing is an area in which she, as a protoindependent young human, is going to make her statement. She'll figure out the rules, "thank you very much a lot." Advice: Wage war elsewhere. Scattered clothes affect neither health nor safety. Just make sure she doesn't freeze her tootsies when you go out because you've left all wardrobe choices up to her.

TIP

113

Toy Death Match

As you glance over from the stove, you see her playing nicely with her Dragontails doll. A few minutes later, she's having Tommy Pickles over with Weezy for a tea party. As the rice is finishing, she's got Weezy and Tommy in a death grip, shrieking, "Bad Tommy! Don't hurt Weezy! You go time-out!"

With a gulp of guilty recognition, you acknowledge that sometimes you come off a little shrill yourself. But this is the third time in two days she's re-enacting her own version of Celebrity Death Match, taking unnaturally gleeful pleasure in the melee.

Chill. This is her way of internalizing the message you've been preaching of getting punished for misbehaviors. She's experimenting by having her friends act badly and playing the mommy who sets the limits and metes out the consequences.

Nothing wrong with that, is there? Putting herself in the role of mommy may even change her ways a little, too.

TIP

114

Transition Zone

No one wants to go home when they're having fun. That's true whether you're a kid or a grownup. For some toddlers, the transition from one activity to the next is invariably met with a standoff.

Sometimes the issue is one of control. He may be attempting to establish the right to take charge of his routine. The more firmly you insist he pack up and go, the further he may dig in his heels.

Other times, the issue may be emotional modulation: He can't break away from something when he's having too much fun. Make periodic announcements: "The train is leaving the station in ten minutes! . . . five minutes! . . . We're putting away our toys now because we're leaving in one minute!"

Finally, look at your own responses. If you lose your temper or become angry, he knows he's going to lose in any case. By withdrawing into himself when you announce "train's leaving," he may be trying to avoid getting yelled at—in a way that is sure to get him yelled at. It's not his fault if you have ten things to do on the way home.

TIP

115

Stranger Shyness

At eight or nine months of age, stranger shyness is perfectly normal and wholly anticipated. By two and a half or three years it's a problem. Solvable, but a problem nonetheless.

A friend of ours had a daughter, Danielle, who would not speak to anyone but her mom or dad. As she was in a preschool at the time, it became a substantial issue: She wouldn't open her mouth to friends or teacher alike.

This "situational anxiety" is common. Danielle, however, had never had a moment of delayed speech. She just decided to clam up. After her parents had her evaluated by behavioral and speech and language specialists, it turned out to be anxiety, and anxiety alone. After some sessions with the child behaviorist, she started opening up more and more in school, and then to other folks around her as well.

Never for a moment was this a language problem, although it can strike a child who has had delays in speaking.

TIP

Nowadays, you see that kid yakking away in the corner at a birthday party? The one whose parents can't shut her up for a second? Yup, that's her.

Fear of Loud Noises

Among the constellation of fears a normal early-toddler develops is *vroomophobia*. Now, my spell-check may have no idea what I'm talking about, but I'm sure you do. It's the startle-and-cry response to the sudden eruption of a vacuum cleaner, a barking dog, a TV or stereo turned on at a roaring volume. (Every family experiences at least once the sonic blast of a stereo whose dials have been twirled by a busy toddler. Next time someone turns it on— *B O O M*—you get a glass-shattering explosion most rock bands can only dream of.)

While you may not be able to completely anticipate oddball events like this, you should be able to arrange vacuuming for when the toddler won't be around, or banish the family pooch to a place where he can bark without being heard. At least until your boy outgrows this transient phobia.

TIP

117

Online Moms and Dads

The World Wide Web is a-changing. At the time of writing, I learned that my favorite parenting site, Moms Online, has downsized pretty hard. No more content, just links and ads. The other giant sites can't quite keep pace, either. I could tell you to type "parenting" or "coping with childhood catastrophes that make me want to tear my hair out" into a search engine, but how are you going to sort through the 10,000 plus responses (sorted by how much advertisers pay to Yahoo! or AOL to promote their site)?

Start with places you know or trust. University children's hospitals provide real services—for preemies, kids with special nutritional needs, post-op care—by people who don't have a vested interest other than caring for patients.

Another good departure point is your government. State health department sites, or national sites such as the National Institutes for Health have what you want from a best friend: objectivity and straight talk. NIAID, for example, the National Institute on Allergy and Infectious Disease has a host of resource tools for parents of allergic or asthmatic kids.

TIP

Measuring Hyperactivity

As a pediatric trainee in Boston, at a clinic for evaluation of hyperactivity, my most memorable encounter was with a thoroughly engaging, sweet-natured, and rambunctious three-year-old. The parents themselves couldn't keep up with him, but his preschool teacher wasn't particularly concerned about hyperactivity. The parents wanted a solution and, I sensed from reading between the lines, medication. The mom was a fatigued forty-four-year-old, and the dad was even more fatigued, his age in the neighborhood of sixty-three.

Our team discussion chewed over the question, When is active *too* active? At what age can a child's activity be considered *hyper*activity? There is no clear answer in medical or behavioral literature, but the consensus seems to be that late toddlerhood (three to three and a half) is probably the lower limit for a meaningful diagnosis. Any younger and the activity style and level are not predictors of how a child's school behavior will be.

TIP

119

It's My Party and I'll Strip if I Want To

We learned to recognize the *look* before the clothes came off. That wild gleam in their eyes (all three of our kids were so stricken) when they suddenly succumbed to the temptation of taking off all their clothes, diaper too, and hurled headlong, naked, into every corner of the house.

This is essentially a no-brainer. They're not hurting anyone, and when they get cold, the clothes go right back on.

Stripping can come at an inconvenient time. Like during a play date or a visit from the pastor. This is when it's time to learn the rules of socially acceptable behavior. No, it's not a safety or acting-out thing, but it's not negotiable, either. When other folks are around, the clothes stay on.

In a few years, age five or thereabouts, the "I'll show you mine if you show me yours" game will be similarly tempting. And that's when they learn the lesson all over again.

TIP

120

Independence Day

The day comes when you hand over the appointment calendar to your little guy. If he wants a play date with a friend or a trip to a museum or the zoo, let him call the shots. Or if he just wants to do an art project, gather together all the material little Mr. da Vinci's going to need. Keep in mind that giving him his freedom does not require compromising the safety and consideration rules.

Successful independence builds a healthy chunk of self-esteem. It can feel like it's backfired, however, when he turns the tables and says "no!" ever more arbitrarily to your plans. Now the rejoinder is *not* "You had your turn, now Mommy needs her turn to decide." Instead, you're into the phase of more reasoned explanation: "We have to get you dressed now so we can go to Grandma's." Or, if he's testing a non-negotiable safety issue: "The doggie is big and he's growling. It's not safe to play with him."

TIP

121

Kitchen Fun: PB & *Fruit* Sandwich

Variations are the spice of life, so why settle for a peanut butter 'n' jelly sandwich when it can be so much more?

Slip a few slices of banana or apple onto a PB-sandwich half instead of jelly. Real fruit has less sugar than jam or jelly and is better nutritionally. Make faces with apple and banana slices and let him trace hair and ears in the peanut butter with his finger.

(Tell him how much Elvis loved banana-and-peanut butter sandwiches!)

Kitchen Fun: Nachos

It's regrettable for a multitude of reasons, but they didn't have nachos when we were kids. Nutritionally, of course, as well as from the grazing perspective, we missed out in a big way. Not so the child of the twenty-first century.

Better still, nachos are a treat even the youngest kitchen helper can achieve. First, spread out a bag of chips on a tray. What self-respecting child would ever refuse a chance to play with chips?

Next, grate the cheese (under close supervision), and sprinkle liberally.

On my nachos, I prefer avocado and tomato to beef and olives, but this is your (and his!) time to get creative.

Add a little lettuce for fiber, peppers for bite, asparagus tips for variety.

Put sour cream on top to hide stuff he might not want to eat if he thought about it.

See? You needn't wait until Super Bowl Sunday to party!

Kitchen Fun: Salad

This advice is so thoroughly wholesome I might never be let into a poker game again, so don't tell anyone.

Have him prepare a dinner salad. Give him a whole, honking-big head of lettuce and let him go to town. Have him shred it as finely as possible, then dump it in the spinner basket and whirl it around. Next, smush in chopped carrots, cukes, celery, tomato . . . the works.

Pour out the right amount of dressing into a container (so he doesn't inadvertently dump a whole bottle's worth), then let him toss. Alternatively, let him create a carrot-cucumber face on a bed of lettuce, and slap the dressing on with a paint (or pastry) brush. This works better with vinaigrette-type dressings, which won't hide his handiwork.

Think of how excited he'll be to eat his own creation! Think of how far this goes to getting you to stick to that diet!

TIP

124

Pro Photography

Sure, you can drop the roll off at the one-hour developer and hope for a good shot. Or the digital camera may let you snap three dozen shots to get one halfway decent picture.

At least once a year, go to a real artist. Film, physical or digital, is nowhere near as sensitive to light as your own eye. Understanding composition, lens lengths, the grain of a film (fine or coarse), or the interplay between extremes of light makes all the difference between a toss-off snap and a work of art.

The semipros like Olan Mills or Sears guarantee a decent portrait, and are not particularly expensive (and what a great gift for Grandma). A real pro photographer costs a lot more, but makes a permanent contribution to your memory book. It's the difference between a nicely posed portrait and a captured instant that tells the story of how you and your little girl or guy really were with each other.

TIP

125

Childproofing: Backyard Smarts

With a magic wand, Mama Nature pulls back the frost and lets spring waft through the air. Do a little exploring in your backyard before letting the young 'uns out.

- Eliminate standing water. A toddler can drown in two inches of water, and in just a few weeks, this can turn into a prime breeding ground for mosquitoes.
- Make a clean sweep for branches that fell in winter, or became half buried in soft, muddy soil.
- Check the deck. Ice and snow may have loosened screws or rotted away planks of wood.
- Garbage patrol: Careless neighbors, or wild animals like foxes or raccoons may have dragged in objects you won't want your toddler exploring, like cigarette butts, broken glass, or raccoon poop.
- It's never too early to be on the lookout for poison ivy. Leaves of three—let them be! The leaves are a brownish green, too, in case you forgot.

TIP

126

Nanny-Gate

Every four years, an incoming presidential administration makes it a point to find a cabinet-level nominee with home-help problems for the sole purpose (scientifically proven!) of reminding you of your own potential Nanny-Gate.

Do you lack proper knowledge regarding what happens if the sitter gets sick or injured on the job? Are you liable? What if she's paid off the books?

In short, anything you do to protect your family and caregiver are going to cost you. As the employer, you may want to take out an insurance policy or buy into workman's comp. Short of that, you might be covered by a liability provision under your homeowner's policy.

If she's paid in a manner that is, say, "IRS invisible," you may want to have a confidential discussion with your insurer to explore ways to rectify the situation.

If she's not a legal citizen, a discreet discussion with a lawyer knowledgeable in the INS's ways is your best bet. Amnesty periods are offered periodically; take advantage of them rather than continue to place everyone at financial and personal risk.

TIP

For Your Bookshelf

Right next to your home medical guide, the video guide, and Scrabble dictionary should be *Every Parent's Guide to the Law* by Deborah L. Forman, a professor on family law (Harcourt Brace, 1998), a readable, user-friendly resource for legal issues in parenting.

Beginning at the beginning, Forman details a pregnant woman's obligation to her fetus, medical care regulations, even laws regarding sperm and egg donation. Urgent issues arising soon after birth—such as matters of taxes and parental workplace rights—usually are, if you're like me, ignored until well into toddlerhood.

Forman takes it all on, giving you the skinny on protecting yourself when things are going smoothly—child care, health, education, guardianship of minors, and financial planning—and what to do when they're not. She highlights everything from child custody rights, visitation, and support/abuse issues to disability education, and options when a parent or parents die.

TIP

The chapter-by-chapter approach to specific legal issues is illustrated with individual cases and bullets to determine when legal counsel is needed. The organization and presentation are clear, even to a legal doofus like me.

128

Summertime Cool-Downs

If you have a backyard pool (a dug-in, pain in the patootie, chemical devouring, equipment-hungry pool, that is) skip this tip. For the rest of us, who have to pack a diaper bag, snacks, change of clothing, stroller, towels, blankets, toys, and sun block just to take a quick dip in the neighborhood pool, try something simpler to help your toddler stay cool with water:

- Water pistols—teeny hand-held ones up to assault-style supersoakers. Never ever aim at the face, in order to avoid high-pressure eye injuries.
- Crazy Daisy. A sprinkler-type system on a floppy length of hose allows the daisy to spray in all directions.
- Your basic, hardware-store-bought, good old American sprinkler. 'Nuff said. Make sure she's wearing flip-flops or sandals.
- A family car-wash.

Avoid flat super-slides or other devices that may let a child propel herself headfirst into a tree or deck. Those are a good way to visit the inside of an ambulance.

TIP

129

Tooth-Friendly (and Unfriendly) Foods

It isn't the sugar, *exactly.* Among the lies and old wives' tales taught to us as children (of the "wait a half-hour before swimming" variety), the "sugar causes cavities" myth has not withstood the test of time and science.

Nowadays, dentists tell us that certain foods are tooth "friendly" or "unfriendly."

Unfriendly: Foods like jam and raisins stick to dental surfaces and gums, and directly lay down sheets of sugar that decay-causing bacteria thrive on. Constant release forms of sugar, like hard candies or a frequently sipped juice bottle, are also no friends of teeth.

FOTs (friends of teeth) include nonsticky foods. Apples and berries contain sugar, of course, but the skins and seeds provide enough abrasion to prevent the sugar from sticking to teeth. Cheese, chocolate, and cashews are beneficial for different reasons. Cheese produces more saliva, which washes teeth; chocolate inhibits plaque from forming; and cashews (a choking hazard, therefore keep this in reserve until about age three) have antibacterial properties.

TIP

130

One-Year-Old Toy: Puzzle

A child mastering the art of eye-hand coordination is fascinating to watch. It's a combination of experimentation, interpretation (of shape, size, and weight), and exploration. You witness all of this firsthand when a one-year-old sits down to explore a puzzle. Her face screws up in fascination as she thinks, "Maybe this upside-down doggie will fit into the right side-up doggie slot if I shove it in hard enough." Then, as the piece rotates a little in her hand, she navigates the consequences of turning it even more until, voila!, it slips into place and won't move anymore. *Oh, yeah, that works!*

She moves on to the piggy and rooster, for the same journey of discovery. Once she memorizes the size and position of all the pieces, she'll still seem to get a charge out of putting them all back in—the right way the first time—just to see it go back together again.

TIP

131

One-Year-Old Toy: Lego

If traditional, wood-block puzzles are classical music, with a rigid beginning, middle, and end in mind, Lego is a jazz riff of endless variations. As the pieces clunk together in new and interesting ways each time, the final product can be a tower in blue, a rainbow coalition, or nothing more than the journey taken.

Lego takes a little more determination, by virtue of the force required to snap the pieces together. It's a statistical certainty that you'll spend all of your time in the evening cleaning the pieces back up, too. And Lego is the habit of a lifetime. As he grows older, Lego grows smaller, and more specific. Plastic and glue airplane or car models of our youth are a vanished breed. Nowadays if you want to make a Star Wars Phantom X-Wing fighter, you do it with Lego kits.

TIP

132

One-Year-Old Toy: Easel

At one, every child is an artist. A two-sided easel is a blank slate for his mind to explore the possibilities of color, texture, and shape. Chalk goes on one side, and a clip for paper on the other lets him create with markers, crayons, and paint.

Of course, you can't expect much more than scribble-scrabble until two or three. So before then, draw something for him and have him help fill in the color, or complete a face with a smile. Take out a favorite book and recreate Maisy or D. W. or Clifford.

Discover—reawaken—your own artistic side.

TIP 133

One-Year-Old Toy: Big Car

Big, bright plastic cars ought to be considered indispensable. Much of what she learns about life begins with imitating Mommy and Daddy, and one of her regular, if not daily activities involves being trundled around in the minivan. So give her the opportunity to drive the places you drive: Aunt Audrey's, the Safeway, the park—all from the convenience of her own playroom.

Does it teach her eye-hand coordination, or socialization skills like taking turns? Nah. Does *that* matter if she's having fun? Nah!

And, hey, these hours may count toward Driver's Ed one day!

TIP

134

One-Year-Old Toy: Hammertime

You find yourself looking at his bright yellow, plastic hammer and peg set, enviously watching him pound the smithereens out of it. You're just waiting for him to wander off to do something else so you can unleash a few whacks on it yourself. You understand the perfection of this $20 toy: What else allows both a one-year-old and a grown-up to attain nirvana?

Toys to Avoid

A nd n-o-o-o-ow, a much needed Mommy moment.

Face it, some toys you just hate. You can only channel those pet peeves internally for so long before something surfaces. But it's okay. You're not alone. In a magazine survey, topping the most-wanted list (for most wanted to melt in the fireplace) was Barbie. Most moms don't even feel particularly threatened that the blonde, anatomically improbable figurine will permanently shape their two-year-old's view of the feminine ideal—they hate the little witch anyway.

Fair enough. So, too, with Barney.

If you don't approve of guns or weapons, ban them from the house.

Also on the dog list: uninspired stuffed animals. A mutt is a mutt is a mutt. Never *ever* overpay for a tie-in doll to this summer's flash-in-the-pan movie. Those may be played with for an hour or two, after that: perma-clutter. Just say no.

TIP

Remember: A stick from the ground can produce a gleam of fascination and fantasy play in a two-year-old, he doesn't need the $30 *Star Wars Episode 2* double-sided light saber to swish around.

The Race to Replace

About once a week or so (just to give the concept a longer shelf life) race her to put away her toys. Let her use a toy shopping cart to go "shopping" for pieces and see who can get the most pieces in the shortest time. Point out carefully, at the start, which toys she's expected to gather up, and with a loud "On your MARK . . . Get SET . . . GO!" you're off. You're going to have to do the straightening up yourself eventually, so make it (marginally) more fun and entertaining, if at all possible, for all concerned.

Panic Buster: Seizures

D on't pry open the mouth or airway of a seizing child. Do not attempt to stop him from biting his tongue. In over a dozen years of general and ER pediatric practice, I have never once seen or heard of a bitten tongue during a seizure. The most important thing to do is to keep him from falling.

Most seizures stop within five to fifteen minutes in all but the most severe situations. During the phase following the shaking and eye rolling, known as a postictal period, the child sleeps it off. If no medications have been given (such as Ativan, Versed, or Valium), this sleep generally lasts no longer than the duration of the seizure itself. In a seizure situation, all you do is call 911 or your doctor.

The big picture: A first-time seizure is a *symptom* of an illness. That is, a fever or infection may cause it. Less often, a change in the body's minerals (such as low calcium or sodium) from vomiting or diarrhea may prompt a seizure. We'll start working on an answer once the seizure has stopped, but please get her to the doctor as soon as you can.

TIP

138

Panic Buster: Objects in Mouth and Throat

If an object inserted in the ear sticks out, attempt to remove it with tweezers. Don't stick anything in the ear below the plane of the skull, as a sudden wrong move can result in a perforated eardrum. Anything fallen completely into the ear requires a doctor, usually an ER or Ear, Nose, and Throat (ENT) specialist, for safe and complete removal.

Objects in the throat go into either the windpipe or esophagus. An episode of coughing, gagging, turning purple or pale followed by milder symptoms of coughing or wheezing means the object has gotten lodged below the windpipe (that's good) and gone into the lung. That's not so good, but not so terrible, either. Endoscopy is needed for retrieval.

A swallowed object stuck in the esophagus either goes straight into the stomach, in which case it magically reappears from the other end the following day, or it remains stuck. Coins, usually nickels and quarters, get stuck in the upper part of the esophagus and cause discomfort but no choking. Once again: Get thee to an ER for endoscopy.

TIP

Electric Shocks: Mini and Mega

It won't shock you to learn there are different kinds of electrical injuries. A shot of static electricity from scuffing across a rug in wintertime or from a battery is a low-level shock of direct current. A minizap. Give Tylenol or Motrin as you would for any other minor boo-boo, cover with antibiotic ointment and a bandage, and apply a cold compress. Sing a song, give a hug.

A lightning strike is a megazap of direct current, but instead of singing and hugging, perhaps you ought to call an ambulance.

A shock from an outlet socket is the other kind of electricity, known as alternating current. Most are completely harmless. If, however, a child is stuck in a socket and writhing in moderate pain, throw a towel around him to pull him away. Don't touch him directly—he could conduct electricity to any rescuer who comes in direct contact. (This is not the case with a lightning strike, even though some folks believe the body becomes dangerously "electrified.") After he's been removed, call 911 and monitor breathing, pulse, and color.

TIP

140

Lice!

At a recent pediatricians' convention in Las Vegas, a study from the Harvard School of Public Health reported that over half of the doctors surveyed made mistakes when trying to identify lice.

The salient point here (aside from the now long-ago—and *forgiven*—rejection of my college and medical school applications) is that if we docs get fooled, so can you.

A louse is a small, brownish, shell-encased object attached firmly to a hair shaft. The big fooler that is *not* lice: big, white, fluffy keratin clumps loosely attached to the hair. Lice lay eggs, which are transferred from best friend to best friend. When one child in a class gets them, all children should be checked.

The best treatment is to cut off all the hair. The second best, most acceptable treatment is permethrin (Nix the 1 percent cream rinse) applied overnight to dry hair, repeated in a week. Combing with a fine-tooth comb is only partially effective. If these treatments fail, check with your doc for plan B.

TIP

141

Panic Buster: Pink Urine

Painless, pink pee-pee is a pure puzzler. Unusual urine hue? Potential explanations are:

- Urate crystals may appear like "brick dust" and though most common in newborns, may result from excess dietary uric acid in older children.
- Beets, berries, and vitamin C discolor urine from excreted food pigments.
- Drugs such as pyridium cause an orange color.
- Urinary infection may look pink, either from blood or from a pigment produced by the bacteria itself.
- Blood in the urine may represent a viral infection (hemorrhagic cystitis) or upper urinary problem such as nephritis (which is accompanied by fever and back pain).
- Kidney stones in children are exceedingly rare, and are always accompanied by severe bouts of crampy pain.

When the Bee Stings!

If it were just a matter of the sting, maybe they wouldn't be so bad, but bees—and wasps, and other members of the genus *hymenoptera*, such as fire ants—deliver a dewdrop of venom, which is what causes problems. Venom is a complex mixture of enzymes that break down proteins and tissues and mediators such as histamine, serotonin, and dopamine. Pretty impressive, huh?

Oh, and more important than all that, they can cause a lightning-fast allergic response. If a sting causes airway problems such as lip/throat swelling, or stridorous (high-pitched, "shrieky") breathing, call 911 immediately and get him to an ER. If you have an epi-pen from previous stings, use it. If the stinger remains in the wound, flick it away to avoid releasing more venom. *Don't pinch.*

Most stings do *not* cause anaphylactic shock. A localized area of redness is not an allergic response: it's a venom reaction. Cool compresses alone are needed, and maybe some antihistamine (like Benadryl). If hives develop, a generalized allergic reaction may be on the way. Make sure your doctor prescribes an epi-pen to have on hand for future bee stings.

TIP

143

Learn CPR

Want to feel really good about yourself? Not just happy-smiley because you've got a wonderful little kid and adoring spouse, but inner-peace-Nirvana serene? Learn CPR, a.k.a. cardio-pulmonary resuscitation. This is *the* tool to possess for confidence in handling the very worst situation that can occur. And it's so remarkably easy to learn.

The rationale is that any child can choke or collapse without warning. When that happens, you must be able to assess the problem and begin to treat it right away—any child, at any time, with no warning.

CPR is simple: Children collapse because of a problem with respiration (a blocked airway or a breathing problem) or circulation (rare heart rhythm disturbances). Whichever reason for the collapse, begin by breathing for the child and pump on the heart to restore circulation.

Once you have mastered this skill, you will never be helpless in a crisis again. Sign up for a CPR course if you've never taken one before. Take a refresher course if it's been a while. Your local hospital/doctor will be able to tell you where to find a course.

TIP

144

Panic Buster: Choking

Managing a choking child is a major part of CPR training.

There are two kinds of choking: complete airway obstruction and partial blockage. In a complete obstruction, the child is unable to cry, cough, or breathe. Have someone call 911 while you do the following:

1. Lay the child on his back.
2. Place the heel of your hand between the belly button and rib cage and *press*, up to five times.
3. Lift the jaw and tongue and remove any objects you see in the mouth.

Keep at it until the obstruction is relieved (and the child starts coughing and breathing) or the child becomes unconscious. If that happens, start mouth-to-mouth breathing and CPR. If you're alone, this is the first opportunity you have to call for help.

In a partial airway obstruction, the child can move air in and out, and will be able to speak or cry, cough and breathe, even if noisily. Do NOT do any of the above maneuvers, since they may turn a partial obstruction into a complete block. Call your doctor or 911.

TIP

When to Call 911

The decision to call for help in a crisis sounds easier on paper than it is in real life. More situations fall into the gray zone of "Is this a crisis?" than not. There are simple guidelines about when to call an ambulance instead of going to the hospital yourself. Even if you *think* you can reach the ER faster, you can't provide any kind of care or help during those few minutes. Call an ambulance when:

- A child collapses and turns blue
- A child is choking—*only* if the child is audibly moving air (If the airway is completely blocked you will have to perform rescue maneuvers yourself! See the Panic Buster for Choking.)
- You suspect a broken bone or neck pain from a serious injury
- A head injury results in an immediate loss of consciousness
- Poisoning is suspected (call the local poison center first)
- A seizure or other change in mental status occurs
- An underlying medical condition fails to respond to usual medications

TIP

146

Kick out the Jams

Weren't we supposed to have *more* time by now? With decades of timesaving devices available to us, wasn't life supposed to be, I don't know, *mellower*? Guess what? It is.

Nature abhors a vacuum, and a lot of the running around we do is getting from one recreational activity to another. Your child's schedule jam (which conflicts with your own jammed agenda, but that's another story) leads you into traffic jams, and brake-jamming when your rushed driving almost gets you into an accident.

If you hit lots of near misses each day, your schedule is too full. You don't need a special play date for each individual friend, or a different class for gymnastics or artwork. If all his activities are therapeutic in one way or another, consider dropping some. He'll figure out how to kick a ball or do somersaults all by himself, or with a little help from Mom or Dad.

TIP

147

Finger Crusher

I try to pass myself off as a tough, seen-it-all ER doc. But an injury that makes me half pass out is the door-crushed fingertip. As far as wounds go, this one looks far worse than it usually is, but boy oh boy, does it ever look awful!

A fingertip caught in a closing door may even come off partially or completely. The good news: reattachment is successful at least 95 percent of the time. Crush injuries to the middle part of the finger are less common and less serious. They may fracture the bone without significant skin damage, and injuries to the lower third of the finger are uncommon.

How to protect against this nasty pitfall: Safety 1st's Finger Pinch Guard (about three bucks, widely available) goes high up on a door and prevents the door from closing. Place them on all the doors through which the wee one passes.

Bicycle Helpers

Having a toddler is no reason to forgo the pleasures of a nice, leisurely bike ride. There are two principle devices: the trailer and the back seat. One is not better than another, per se, and each has advantages and disadvantages.

Trailers are expensive, at least $250 new. They don't tip over unless you go over a large rock or curb. Even then, the child is (a) low to the ground, and (b) strapped in securely enough to escape injury. A disadvantage to trailers is *weight*. These suckers are heavy, and peddling up even the slightest rise is a chore. A great workout, but work you will.

Carrier seats are cheaper, lighter, and offer a much better view for your passenger. Newer models have side and head protection, so a fall is less hazardous. The big downside: the center of gravity is much higher, making the bike less stable. It takes a few rides to adapt. My advice: The carrier is for stronger, more experienced riders. Go for the trailer if you're a worrier, or a less sure-footed cyclist.

Caution: Always ride with a child on hiker-biker trails or other auto-free paths. Car drivers are idiots. With cell phones.

TIP

Discipline: Time-Outs

Some days you'll give half a dozen time-outs, some days will pass without a one. But have it ready when all else fails. Keep it easy and simple: you've said no (*one*), you mean no (*two*) and now there are no more chances (*three*)!

One minute of time-out per year of age is a good rule of thumb, as this closely matches a toddler's attention span. Sit him in a corner where he can fidget but do little else. No toys, no friends, no rewards other than sitting and not having fun.

Remember to keep it positive afterward. Tell him you love him, remind him that he had a couple of chances to stop doing a bad or dangerous behavior, and that you know he's capable of good behavior. Seal it with a kiss and an "I love you." Then it's back to hoping that the time-out made a difference.

TIP

150

Discipline: Losing Privileges

The threat of losing a privilege goes a step beyond using a time-out to discipline. She must be old enough to understand that losing a video or play date later on is a consequence of an action she can remember from the morning. This takes the attention span and understanding of at least a three year-old. Telling an eighteen-month-old that she can't have a reward an hour from now is meaningless.

"I Heard You, Dear."

When he wants that box of cookies in the market, and tells you over and over (*"Wan coo-kee! WAN cooKEE!"*) register that you heard his complaint. Repeat it back to him: "Mommy knows you want the cookies, but we're not buying them right now."

His receptive language skills are there. He'll hear you, he'll understand you, even if he then proceeds to dig down into his deepest powers and holler, *"WAN COO-KEE!!!!"*

If possible, allow him to buy his way back to the bargaining table. Remind him (he's listening even if he's not demonstrating it) that he's not to yell, and if he quiets down, acts properly, and asks the best way he knows how, he may be able to earn the cookies. Appealing to his better nature may lessen his frustration, and give him a chance to argue his case one more time.

TIP

152

Bad Habits: Nail Biting

The Shining was a nail-biter. Your little Sammy shouldn't be. But don't be too hard on him if he is. Nail biting can start with an irregular or torn nail. He tries to even it up and then may go on to the next finger, and the next. It's the perfect accompaniment to a lazy morning of TV shows. When they get bored in other venues— the car seat, the stroller—they return to this lazy pastime. Bitten nails can become infected, and they can tear through the finger or part of the nail. Ouch.

This habit is best busted by lying low. Ordering him to stop only draws more attention, and it's mainly when his attention drifts that his hand drifts mouthward. He shouldn't be blamed as if it were a conscious decision. Cut and file the nails regularly so he has less to work with. Use lotion if his fingers are dry; apply polish and a hardener for girls.

TIP

153

Mystifying Habits: Teeth Grinding

Somewhere around the age of eighteen to twenty-four months certain children develop the weirdest habit of all: bruxism. Teeth grinding. It occurs exclusively during sleep. No one knows why. Typically, the situation develops like this: Dad goes into Nathan's room to kiss him good night and discovers him grinding away. He calls Mom in, but by the time she's off the phone, Nathan has stopped and she tells Dad he's imagining things. Next night, same thing. Ditto the following night. Eventually Mom sees Nathan grimacing away herself and immediately calls the dentist. Months later, they get a bill for $185 (all of which goes to the deductible) for his shrug-casual diagnosis: "Bruxism, it's normal."

There's no treatment for teeth grinding, since it never results in tooth or jaw malocclusion. Remember this tip and save yourself some money!

Disgusting Habits: Nose Picking

Here's the wrong way to stop nose picking: "Oh, stop that *gross* digging!" accompanied by a face worthy of Jim Carrey in a more rubbery moment. Here's why it's the wrong way to stop nose picking. Your child's response to the above: "Watch me *eat* it!" Followed by ingestion of the picked piece of mucus.

Fact of life: Children eat their boogers. They do, they do, they do.

Pick from the list why it's a problem: socially unacceptable, efficiently transfers cold and flu germs to toys and other siblings/playmates, causes nosebleeds and impetigo.

Here's the correct way to limit nose picking (you may not win this battle until he's five or six): offer a tissue and help him to blow his nose, if needed. Humidify the room, especially at night to halt the drying out of stuff that accumulates overnight. Apply a little lip balm or petroleum jelly to the nostrils to lock moisture in his skin. Don't make faces when he does it.

TIP

155

Exasperating Habits: Lip Licking

A ri, the lion in winter, grows an extra set of lips. From sucking and licking his primary set of lips, that is. Contrary as it sounds, saliva is drying. Constantly mouthing or licking lips, especially when in arid winter air, leads to chapped lips. The seeming solution, if you're two, is to lick them some more to moisten them up.

And thus, a rim of red secondary lips.

Aside from the vicious and cyclical nature of the problem, this also leads to impetigo, a minor bacterial skin infection. Impetigo, however, can spread further. Lip balm is the best, surest way to stop licking. Reapply several times during the day. Watch out, as some balms sting more than others. Don't create unnecessary battles; find one that works. Hard, waxy Chap Stick may work better than moist, mushy Vaseline. Reapply at night, while she's asleep. This heals lips fastest.

TIP

156

Masturbation

I trust you know the drill by now. Exploration of body parts, which begins in infancy, eventually leads to discovery of the penis or vagina. Appropriate response: Ignore the social inappropriateness, instruct them to do it in private, that it is not done in front of other people. Exploration of sibs' or playmates' genitals is not appropriate, either.

Inappropriate response: expressions of outrage, embarrassment, mortification, physical punishment. Masturbation is innocent, developmentally appropriate, normal behavior. With time, toddlers will turn their interest to other activities.

TIP

157

Hair Pulling

Another tough call from the pages of a pediatrician's advice magazine has to do with hair pulling. An eighteen-month-old was twirling his hair so much that he had unsightly bald patches. He had no other "rhythmic" behaviors like rocking or head banging, and the twirling was worst at bed and naptime. The advice: First recognize that this is a tough habit to break, and you could be in for a long haul.

Next, tackling the habit comes down to distracting the child and seeking to engage his hands and attention in other ways. A hand sock loosely attached to the wrist may work if the child doesn't become too agitated at losing control. Cutting the hair is reasonable for boys, but poses more of a problem for girls. Finally, though messy, apply some petroleum jelly to the hair if absolutely nothing else works. This could take a few tries, but might provide the necessary deterrent.

TIP

158

Pulling Her Hair Out, Literally

We grown-ups talk about pulling out our hair far more often than we actually do so. The opposite is true with children. They don't make a big deal about it; they just do it. There is greater occurrence with girls than boys, because tickly long hair touching the face can be an ever-present reminder.

Usually the habit starts by absentminded hair twirling, then tugging on it for a more intense sensation. Harder tugs follow until she can yank on it with little pain or outcry. It may start out as an exploratory behavior but often ends up as a nervous, worrying gesture, often accompanied by thumb or finger sucking.

Cutting her hair short is one way to short-circuit the problem. Drastic, but effective. The best behavior modification is to investigate what situations bring on the nervousness (and offensive habit) and deal with them.

If her hair begins falling out in patches *without* her pulling at it, she's got a condition known as alopecia. Take her to a doctor for an evaluation.

TIP

159

Teaching Numbers

A colleague of mine, also an ER pediatrician, taught numbers to her two-year-old, Emma, by having her call Mom at work. "Find the 2!" *Beep*! "Find the 1" *Boop*. "Find the 2 again!" *Beep*! In no time at all, Emma learned her numbers and also learned how to run up the phone bill. "Wanna make-a nutha call!" To Daddy's office, to Grandma, to Singapore (when she forgot to ask for help with the numbers) . . . Keep an eye on her while she "practices."

TIP

160

One-and-a-Half-Year-Old Toy: Memory

Memory card games are hugely fascinating to toddlers, once they have the capacity to play—as early as about eighteen months. Start with two or three pairs of cards, and add more as they get better. This helps to teach and reinforce concepts of shape and color, and can be a good way to introduce him to his numbers and letters as well. Don't be too surprised if his memory turns out to be better than yours: At three or four years old, playing with thirty or forty cards, his concentration and recall can equal any adult's. And don't blame your loss on being distracted by watching the baby.

TIP

161

Travel Tip: Eyes in the Back of Your Head

The rear-facing back-seat passenger is out of sight and, I bet, out of mind when you get wrapped up on the cell phone. Stick a mirror on the back seat and aim it for your rear view mirror. You can find them in stores or make your own. It comes in handy when you're on a sick visit to the pediatrician. I've heard not a few stories of children having febrile seizures while en route to the doc. The mirror also helps monitor their breathing during an asthma attack.

In less dire circumstances, a mirror makes for a way to keep an eye on their boredom or fussy level. When they fall asleep, you'll know this is the reason why he's *too* quiet.

TIP

162

Trampoline Fence

As a licensed professional who treats injuries daily, I see the hazards and risks in any activity a child might conceivably regard as fun. As a daddy, I watch my child engage in these activities and think, "Cooool!" or, "I used to do that, too."

To bridge the gap between these warring instincts, I look for devices that allow kids to have fun while limiting needless dangers. Which leads me to the trampoline. Not only is a trampoline a ton of fun, an activity I look back on with great fondness, but it is also, alas, a uniquely hazardous sporting apparatus. I've seen permanent brain damage and horrific neck injuries resulting in quadriplegia to children who missed a landing or jumped wrong.

Thank goodness for Jump Sport. They designed a mesh-net fence that completely encloses a trampoline and vastly diminishes terrible risk. If you own a trampoline at home, shell out the $150 or so to buy peace of mind (spend less if you can find one on eBay). Lobby your school's gym, and lobby them hard, to buy it. Remind them that just settling the lawsuit will cost dozens of times more than even the top-of-the-line model of Jump Sport.

TIP

163

Travel Tip: Edible Accessories

A car tip that kills two avians with one geoform is the old edible accessory trick.

Make a Cheerios necklace or fruit roll-up watchband before the trip. If you can get him to resist eating it as soon as you take off, you have one less thing to do (such as digging through the bag to get the snack out) while at the red light.

When to Let Him Get Away with It

Rules are rules, but then again rules are meant to be broken. And aren't there exceptions to every rule? There are, generally speaking, but when is it *safe* to let your darling Alexander get away with an infraction?

Most behaviorists probably draw the line at age three. That's an age at which many of the rules of safety, manners, and consideration are firm enough so that the occasional lightening up won't threaten the overall scheme of the universe.

Then, make sure that the rules you're bending are appropriate. It *is* okay to jump on the bed or sofa sometimes, if there's no glass table nearby or flimsy table lamps to knock over. Food is to be eaten in the kitchen only, except when she's really earned a TV snack. Keep it safe, and keep consideration in mind and you won't go too far afoul of the law.

TIP

165

Shyness

Klingon. Velcro. Timmy Timid.

Some children are just naturally shy. They prefer the solitary company of a parent or caregiver to a raucous birthday party or a hectic playground. Such children are generally quite happy—in the right circumstances. Do's and don'ts:

- Do encourage participation even in busy situations. It may be a stretch to join in with half a dozen noisy kids, but let her know you're close at hand. Reassure her that she can come to you for a mental moment after ten or fifteen minutes.
- Don't criticize or ignore the withdrawal instinct. She is who she is, and failure to acknowledge that can only increase her anxiety.
- Do her a favor and try to arrange single-friend play dates, where there is less opportunity for roughhousing and out-of-control zaniness.
- Don't worry. Every shy kid has her place in the world.

TIP

166

Just Fun Books: Eric Carle

The works of an artist for every age and interest. Indulge in.

- *The Very Hungry Caterpillar:* Growth, transformation, and very interesting dietary choices.
- *The Very Busy Spider:* A primer in zoology, Darwinism, and the work ethic.
- *Papa, Please Get the Moon for Me:* Monica wants the moon, but it's so-o-o big. Daddy obliges her.
- *Dragons, Dragons* and *Animals, Animals:* Mythological and mysterious creatures as they've never been done before. A keeper—for the grownups.

TIP

167

Reading Games

At bedtime, reading should be passive, quiet, soothing. The rest of the time, it's a game:

- Talk about the pictures: What is the birdie doing? Count stars in the sky, compare cows from book to book.
- Let her turn pages: Have her follow along to gain word or letter recognition, build fine motor skills.
- Substitute names: Thing One and Thing Two from *The Cat in the Hat* can make a magical appearance in *Curious George*, or Madeline pays D. W. a visit. (I always thought they'd get along great, although Madeline might have her hands quite full with the pesky little sister . . .)

TIP

168

The Fluoride Thing

Fluoride helps form dental enamel, the hard stuff that makes teeth so strong. A little is good, too much causes fluorosis: mottling and irregular white spots on the teeth. In severe cases, they can make teeth brittle and weak. What's up with fluoride, anyway?

Fluoridation of water is generally sufficient to protect teeth. On the other side of the coin, swallowing too much toothpaste can lead to vomiting and fluorosis. For these reasons, a couple of fluoride-free toothpastes are available on the store aisles right up there with Crest and Colgate.

Do you need fluoride? Should you be worried about the possibility of excess fluoride intake? If you live in an area that does not fluoridate water or drink exclusively from bottled water, your child should not use fluoride-free pastes. But if you live in an area with fluoridated water, it doesn't matter one way or the other. If you find your little guy sneaking off to lick or taste the toothpaste frequently, then it probably pays to limit his fluoride availability.

TIP

169

High-Tech Tooth Care

Unlike the days of our childhood, when we used a single toothbrush for an entire presidential administration, you need to replace a brush every four to six months. It's not that they are shoddy now, but after a few months, the bristles get, well, *mangy*. New bristles brush teeth clean.

It amounts to criminal negligence to buy a plain-vanilla brush for your child. When you have choices ranging from Barbie to Yoda, why would you *ever* buy a characterless brush? (Oh, maybe because they're cheaper.)

At the head of the brush, there are shape and texture options. Soft and small are better, with incrementally bigger heads as your kid grows. The more strokes you give to each tooth, the cleaner they'll be. Clearly, then, high-tech battery-powered brushes with rotating brush heads do the best job. Reach, Sonicare, and Interplak manufacture a family-wide selection. The base unit costs more than the average brush, but just one serves a whole family. Replace brush heads as often as you would a regular brush, and that also costs a little more.

No kid *needs* a motorized brush, but the process is more fun, which may result in healthier teeth and lower dental bills.

Kid-Friendly Dentists

Remember back when you had to choose a pediatrician? You could choose between a family practitioner or a pediatrician. Well, here you go again. A general, family-care dentist can care for your child's teeth as well as a pediatric dentist in many cases. The choice is yours.

After all, kids' teeth should be healthy and need minimal checking. Practically speaking, the biggest difference between a dentist who serves a kid and a family practice is the number of dinosaur and cartoon stickers on the walls. Find someone you trust who has a staff that enjoys caring for kids. If you run into problems above and beyond simple cavities or routine care issues, make sure the dentist is comfortable managing such problems, if not, she can refer you to someone else.

Just as in test-driving a car, don't get too distracted with the nonessentials. Games, stickers, and rewards are all well and good, but the under-the-hood, critical element is how well the dentist examines and cleans children's teeth. If the hygienist is rushed and rough, take a hike. If the staff won't help you with insurance or billing questions, give 'em a long, lingering look at your back as you leave.

TIP

171

Floss Is Your Friend

You're off the hook, floss-wise, until fifteen to eighteen months, when molars appear. Flossing removes bacteria between teeth. When teeth abut each other, a toothbrush cannot get in to remove germs, and therefore, the first cavities often appear in molars where teeth lie right next to each other. Sit him in your lap, once he's ready, and take a small piece of floss. Come from over the top of the head, just as the dentist sits over your head while rooting around in your mouth, for the best angle to watch where you're going. A couple of passes will do. Since there aren't that many teeth to begin with, you don't need to spend much time flossing. Unless, of course, he's the county squiggle champion.

TIP

172

Dirt Diet

Philip and Lilyan, those loveable Rugrats, have a way with, um, gross-outs. One must offer kudos to the brilliant animators who manage to capture the delighted look of curiosity and anticipation as Lil picks up a yummy, wormy morsel and Phil hopes for a taste.

Okay, maybe your little Phil and Lil don't actually eat bugs, but what about dirt? Is there any harm in eating what's on the ground?

The perils are few but worthy of attention. First, lead in soil is highest near major roadways (because there are still trucks around that may use a higher-lead diesel fuel). Recently developed suburbs (any development after, say the mid-seventies) should be relatively lead free.

Second, germs are more likely to be picked up where wildlife abounds. If a lot of dogs roam your child's favorite park, the soil is higher in E. coli and other fecal bacteria. Chemicals and physical hazards like broken glass are far less common dangers on the list. Bottom line on eating dirt: medium to low danger, high to extreme gross-out—and that may be the whole point.

TIP

173

Candy Crazes—and Crazies

Do sugar, caffeine, and chocolate cause mood and behavior changes? In a nutshell, no, yes, and no. Diet and behavior studies have reported the following conclusions:

- Sugar: Kids' activity levels before and after a dose of high-sugar foods failed to show any differences to both parents and objective observers.
- Caffeine: A study involving 250 children allowed them to drink a soda with 50 milligrams of caffeine (typical for a twelve-ounce can). The result: a passel of irritable, jumpy kids who all had headaches when they withdrew from the study.
- Chocolate: Studies seem to agree that excess jitteriness or hyperactivity following a massive chocolate intake is due to caffeine or other additives.

TIP

174

KidCam

The Truman Show and *Ed TV* were movies in a time, back in the quaint old twentieth century, when the idea of living one's life entirely under the watchful eye of a video monitor was unnerving and Big Brother-ish.

We modern, shiny, bright, twenty-first-century folk, however, love our e-toys. More and more day care centers and preschools offer Web-cam access to view, in real-time, Danny's daily doings from your workplace. The monetary costs may be passed along in the form of higher tuition, or may be offset by higher enrollment. But are there other costs? Is it going to make your child suspicious, always being under surveillance? Or is he going to grow up nervous if someone isn't keeping a close eye?

According to magazine surveys, most parents feel positive about the opportunity to stay connected. A live-cam inhibits opportunities for child molesters, and exposes folks who have an unhealthy curiosity in their child's activities.

It's your call. It's a brave new world out there.

TIP

175

Miss Manners 2

Miss Manners:

Mark is two, and we were in the park yesterday. A woman from the nearby assisted living center offered my son a cookie while I was nursing the baby. I don't think she's the kind of person to hurt a child, but I want him to learn the rules about not accepting candy from strangers.

What am I to do?

Dear Shrinking Violet:

If I were to guess, I'd say you also have trouble talking down Grandma when she wants to offer Mark a lavish present, no? The sweet elderly, woman offering your son a treat is probably very familiar with the "don't–accept–candy–from–anyone–you–don't–know" warning. Warmly thank her for her consideration and explain that your son isn't old enough to discriminate between well- and ill-intentioned strangers.

TIP

Starting at about eighteen months, a child is ready to understand that it's bad to accept candy from strangers. Rather than teaching him through fear, make it a matter of manners by instructing him to say, "I need to ask Mommy." That is, if you can get him to inhibit the grab reflex.

Birthday Party Tips

If you drive yourself gonzo for her first or second birthday party, how are you ever going to cope with really big deals like graduation or confirmation?

Unless you're Donald Trump, keep it short, sweet, and cheap.

Short: Plan on an hour to ninety minutes for a first- or second-year-old's party, two to two and a half hours for a three- or four-year-old's party. More than that and you'll have contagious meltdown on your hand: Katie will cry because Megan is crying, who's crying because Hannah is wailing . . .

Snacks: Pizza or PB sandwiches and ice cream. Do children ever tire of these?

Cheap: Any costs over $75 means you're being taken for a ride.

TIP

177

Birthday Party Themes

Keeping up with the Wexlers is a direct ticket to ulcers. They rented a Moonbounce? Fuggeddabouddit. The Hammers had a live animal show? Let them clean up the mess.

Your toddler's favorite activities and characters are your starting cue. Is he into sports? Make a play-ball party where all the kids get to have a chance to shoot a (kiddie) hoop, play putt-putt, kick a soccer ball. Into the arts instead? Have them do their own painting project—paint a rock or sunglasses and let them take it home as their "goody bag."

If you're feeling ambitious, line up a half-dozen friends for a trip to the children's museum or zoo. Be sure to sign up a few chaperones to keep the head-count headaches down.

Goody-Bag Ideas

Cynics (such as dads, but certainly not *me!*) might point out that birthday party gift bags are nothing more than unneeded junk food or worthlessly cheap toys that end up as landfill within twenty-four hours of the party's end.

They might (I'm speculating wildly, here) also point to evidence suggesting that children end up being more miserable (they left it at the party with their hat and gloves, the older sib didn't get one too, it spilled, the toy *isn't working!*) than happy with the goody bag. Such Scrooge-ish folks might make a deal with all their friends and families: No useless, waste-of-time-and-money items for all their parties so that no one feels jealous or left out.

Not that you'd ever hear that from me, but be on the lookout! There are churlish, self-centered, un-fun-loving parents out there who think it's better to spend the time and money it takes putting together gift bags doing one-on-one things with their kids, instead. Go figure!

TIP

179

Party Idea: Field Trip

Nontraditional birthday parties get harder and harder to come up with. Thanks go to my socially conscious niece Hannah for this one.

Take your friends to an animal shelter and make friends with friendless pups and kitties. Maybe someone will adopt one of those big-eyed, slobbery mutts. Tell all the moms and dads that instead of goody bags, you're going to make a donation to the shelter on the children's behalf. Better yet, have them each give their child a dollar to contribute during the visit. When the child is the one to make the big gesture of Giving, it will have more impact than a thousand recitations of why it is better than Receiving.

Alternate field trips: fire and rescue station, recycling center, police station. Children (in organized groups) are more welcome than you may realize, and most people love to talk about what they do for a living.

TIP

180

Terrible Twos: I Hate You!

Remember when, during the bright-eyed, commando-crawling ninth month, you wondered what she would say if she could? Now that she's two, try to keep that hopeful memory front and center when, exhausted and cranky at the end of her rope (her, that is, not you) she barks out, "I hate you! I hate you!"

What's up with that? Of course she doesn't hate you. But if, exhausted and cranky at the end of your rope (yes, you), this is all you get for a marathon of patience and tidying up after Hurricane Annie, you might need convincing.

It's just another step in the social development cycle. That's all. And tell that to your partner when, exhausted and cranky at the end of his rope (he's had a rough day, too), she barks out, "I hate you! I hate you!" when all he's done is try to keep her from running into the stove and hurting herself.

She's just expressing frustration and fatigue. Honest.

TIP

181

Stuttering

A round the age of two or two and a half, an odd misstep takes place, even in the most articulate of toddlers. A normally confident, expressive child begins to hesitate and trip over the simplest of sentences.

What gives? Is it stuttering or a speech delay?

Most likely neither. Like a record stuck on a track (a concept I'm sure to have to explain in another ten years or so), some children hesitate over finishing a thought or naming an object. It starts out as a rare event but then becomes more common over the next few weeks.

For the most part, this stammering goes away as gradually as it came. It merely indicates his mind is racing past what his mouth is saying, and may not quite know how to resynchronize the two.

If the problem extends into self-frustration or aggravation over inability to make himself understood, it is worth having a doctor or speech therapist listen in. A useful ally to help you reality-check is his preschool teacher. He or she is pretty keenly tuned into real problems versus passing stages.

TIP

182

Speech Difficulties

Between eighteen and twenty-four months, a child's verbal communication is generally comprehensible only to his mom and dad. Between two and two and a half, though, most other adults should be able to make out what he's saying. If, at this age, Mom and Dad aren't even sure what he's saying, the situation ought to be evaluated.

Some children at this age are quiet and avoid speaking. The great majority of such children won't turn out to have a real language problem, but this situation deserves evaluation and perhaps behavior therapy.

A child who shows no ability to follow simple instructions or carry out commands at two and a half is in need of a speech-language evaluation.

Children who lisp or substitute consonants inappropriately may have, at worst, articulation difficulties. These, too, respond quite nicely to speech therapy.

TIP

183

How to Take Medicine

The first, and absolutely hands-down, most important rule of giving medicine is not to hesitate giving the medicine. Those sharp little creatures known as toddlers can smell indecision a mile away and instinctively use every tactic to play on that reluctance. This alone resolves half of all battles. As for the other half:

- A few extra degrees of chill will eliminate some of the sour taste.
- With few exceptions, most common drugs these days are available in once- or twice-daily dosing. Push your doc on this, and then research it. Internet sites like WebMD and most parenting sites let you research alternatives.
- Push and pull. Draw his thirst with some chips ahead of time, follow the medication with a chaser: cold juice or water.
- Some medications are available as a suppository—a last-ditch solution when all else fails.

TIP

184

Asthma Devices

Since just about every self-respecting asthma medication works better in the airway than in the bloodstream, a Metered Dose Inhaler (MDI) is the way to go.

However, MDIs take some coordination, and while breath activated devices make their way to market, children under five will need . . .

- Spacers: With or without a facemask. For younger toddlers and even infants, the holding device contains the MDI spray inhaled breath by breath. It takes up to six breaths to get all (or most) in.
- Dry Powder Inhalers (DPI): The medication starts as a tablet and is broken up by the force of inhalation. They may not break up the pills as effectively into breathable particles.
- Nebulizers: Noisy but effective. Hooked up to a home oxygen supply, you get the best of both worlds, since oxygen alone relaxes tight bronchi.

TIP

Making Sense of: Cough Medications

Kids cough! Cold cough? Croupy cough? Chronic cough? Cruddy cough! What a lot of coughs there are. (Apologies to Dr. Seuss.) What a lot of cough *drugs* there are!

- Codeine is the only cough medicine that really works. Most doctors are reluctant to prescribe it because of extreme drowsiness—and it's a narcotic.
- Guaifenesin is an expectorant; it loosens up mucus in the back of the throat, making it easier to expel (*Ptuiiii!*). Medications containing guaifenesin are usually named "–tuss," or "Guai-" or have a "-G" suffix. They're only moderately effective, but they are generally free of serious side effects.
- Dextromethorphan is a non-narcotic version of codeine. It's about as effective as guaifenesin. (A tip-off for dextromethorphan is the suffix "-DM.")

Making Sense of: Cough Medicine Warnings

There are two coughs you should not try to stop. Coughing due to pneumonia or wheezing/Reactive Airway Disease.

In pneumonia, a collection of fluid fills a portion of the lung. Suppressing a cough with codeine interferes with the body's efforts to rid itself of the bacteria and fluid. Even the limited effect from a -DM (dextrometorphan) medication is undesirable. Antibiotics are the mainstay of treatment for pneumonia, but guaifenesin may help break up the thick congestion rising from the lungs.

Coughing from asthma or bronchiolitis is caused by constriction of air passages inside the lung. The appropriate medication (albuterol, Atrovent) dilates these air passages. It does not suppress the cough.

If, after all your struggles, the medications aren't working, throw 'em away. You're attempting to provide symptomatic relief, and all these drugs do is complicate matters by adding side effects. Mucus and (mild) coughing serve an important function: expelling the bad humors from your child, and letting Mother Nature do her job.

TIP

187

The No-Nonsense Posture

So when you've yelled yourself blue in the face and chased her around the house until you've run a full marathon, it's time for the secret weapon.

Standing straight in front of the misbehaving little culprit, shoulders squared, bending slightly at the hip (so you're *in* her face), laser-beam in on her eyes. Let her wait and wonder what's next. Understand the power of silence. It has to end *sometime*, and when it does something's gonna happen . . .

Hold the posture a moment or two longer (but not enough to let her start playing around, which might test your resistance to giggling). This is, frankly, an intimidating stance, one more properly suited to a mob shakedown. But it accomplishes the task of telling her she's gone too far.

Once you have her undivided attention, tell her the exact nature of the crime and what the punishment will be. Then carry it out.

TIP

188

Headache

Unlike a tummy ache, a headache is somewhat infrequent in toddlers, and the younger they are, the rarer it is. Many times a headache in a toddler comes from a head bonk that you might not otherwise know about. Another important consideration is that fever from a minor illness can produce headaches. If so, it gets better quickly when the temp comes down.

Sometimes a toddler says his head hurts when what he really means is that he has a sore throat, earache, or sinus infection.

The really awful, bad stuff, a brain tumor or meningitis is rarely heralded by just a headache. A brain tumor comes on as morning-time headaches relieved by forceful vomiting. This is progressive over the course of weeks. Meningitis also may have headache as an early feature, but more often it is overshadowed by such symptoms as neck stiffness, pain from looking at bright lights, and very high fever.

TIP

189

Earache

Not all earaches are ear infections. At least as common as *otitis media* (the diagnostic name appearing on your doctor bill for a simple ear infection), pressure from congestion in a common cold blocks the passageway connecting the middle ear and back of the throat.

Erupting molars cause earaches, as does a strep throat. An outer ear infection, *otitis externa*, causes earaches, too, and the ear hurts when it's touched or otherwise bothered.

On occasion, the little one's ever-active hands and wondering mind will place a small toy in the ear, perhaps with the intention of pushing it all the way through to the other side. Unsuccessful experiments like this bring about the painful and sometimes difficult-to-manage problem of ear foreign bodies, but at least that's not as gross as the occasional insect that crawls into the ear and can't get out.

TIP

190

Tummy Ache

A toddler's tummy ache is a tough beast to pin down. It can be a singularly vague, common complaint. It can mean anything from constipation to migraine. "I suspect," as Inspector Clouseau would say, "*everyone!*"

A tummy ache signifies a real problem when accompanied by fever, vomiting, listlessness, or blood from the mouth or rear end. Mostly, a sudden complaint of a stomachache indicates a minor intestinal virus or constipation. Far less often, when a stomachache gets progressively worse and worse, diagnoses such as appendicitis, intussusception (an intestinal problem), and other unusual diagnoses, such as a disorder known as HSP, must be considered. Every now and then, a throat infection with strep is the cause of tummy ache. Think UTI (Urinary Tract Infection) in a girl with a lower abdominal pain and (usually but not always) pain on peeing.

As an isolated symptom it can be baffling and can be long term if it becomes an attention-seeking complaint. Don't play around. See a doctor, and accept the possibility that no specific cause may be found.

TIP

191

Nosebleeds

Probably all children experience a nosebleed at least once before turning five. Most bleeds begin with free-flowing, bright red blood and end less than ten minutes later. Causes:

- Nose picking
- Dry weather
- Colds, especially in children on antihistamine and decongestant medications
- Rebound from coming off decongestant cold medications
- Any or all of the above in combination (which is why so many kids get them)

Children with recurrent nosebleeds may have a minor clotting abnormality known as von Willebrand's disease. This is a disorder of the platelets (which act as a blood component to promote clotting). It is *not* hemophilia. Some kids with von Willebrand's have frequent or prolonged nosebleeds, and a medication known as DDAVP helps to lower the duration and frequency.

TIP

192

Nosebleed Management

Nosebleeds get messy even if you manage them carefully, so try to do exactly as follows:

1. First, have your child lean forward. This lets the blood flow out of the nose instead of down the back of the throat.
2. Do not tilt his head backward. This allows blood to flow down the back of the throat and into the stomach, and he'll vomit dark, nasty-looking blood.
3. Pinch the nose. Pressure stops blood flowing from the open capillary bed, and allows clotting.
4. Keep pressure on for at least ten minutes. Blood clotting takes at least this much time.
5. Use a cold compress or ice pack to continue to restrict blood flow.
6. Apply Vaseline to the outside of the nostrils to cover the dry mucous membranes and prevent another episode.
7. Clean the mess up. Use hydrogen peroxide to get bloodstains out of clothing.

TIP

193

Head Injury Tactics

Inevitable as the anvil dropping on Wile E. Coyote is the sudden thud of your toddler against something even more solid in the next room. A pause, then a wail, heartrending and helpless.

Keep your head. That pause between impact and the first cry is *not* a loss of consciousness, but only that moment it takes for him to process the information of a fall, register it as pain, and vocally respond to it. If he has hit his head, he ought to settle down in ten to twenty minutes, and then he'll want to take a nap. This is normal. Let him. If he sleeps briefly, wakes up, and acts his normal self, he's fine and dandy. If he throws up once or twice? Still okay. When he has a more prolonged loss of consciousness, or vomits more than two times, it's time to call your doctor.

TIP

194

Common Rashes

Pictures are worth a thousand words, so open up your home medical reference to familiarize yourself with these common rashes.

- Ringworm: Raised, round bumps, pink or without any special coloration. They can be from dime-sized to quarter-sized.
- Eczema: Flaking, scaly patches, often red. These are scattered on the cheeks, behind the ears, inside the knees and elbows.
- Impetigo: Spreading, red blisters with a honey-colored fluid inside. These are only moderately itchy.
- Molluscum contagiosum: Pearly, tiny firm blisters with a central notch. These appear singly in a scattered distribution.

TIP

195

Toilet Language

A confession: I use bad words. My children were horrified the first time a banned word slipped out, and even more thunderstruck at my silent acquiescence to songs with such words. I would argue, however, that the majestic English language reserves a special role for taboo words. Furthermore, with few exceptions, we've all engaged in this trash talk at one time or another.

So how hard do you come down on your two-year-old when he says at the dinner table, "I want !$#@! peas, Mommy"? As in the case of, "Hey, that guy's *fat!*" the lesson is that there is a time and a place for all kinds of speech, but it's not respectful for children to use those words. Period. Not just around adults, but around other toddlers. It's wrong. Don't do it. No way, Jose. The issue will resurface in kindergarten and then in every grade thereafter. At some point along the line, they will be talking the talk with their friends—but by then, you can hope they know the limits.

TIP

196

Slowpokes

How come some kids can bolt down dinner inside of three seconds and other kids can't finish a hot dog in three hours?

Please e-mail me when you find out, and I'll pass it along to the Nobel committee. They are, I hear, quite interested in tracking down a cure for this inexplicable phenomenon.

Until then, you're almost on your own for answers. You may attempt to regulate the oral input of a twenty-month-old by offering incentives and speedy rewards. But don't expect miracles.

And don't let a child go hungry. If you have to get going and he still has not finished eating, don't punish him with hunger because he hasn't eaten his fill. Given that *you're* going to suffer just as greatly (from the crying and whining *and* pangs of guilt), the solution is simply to bring the remaining food along in a baggie.

Quality Doc Time

Modern medical care these days can be summed up in the following mantra: "Not enough time," which applies to both sides of the examining table. If you have trouble getting your doctor to spend time discussing your concerns, it may be because his network limits him to x number of minutes per patient. It's not uncommon to have bean counters insist that if the docs don't plow through six or seven patients per hour, sick visit or well, they're gonna go under. Not that they're *telling* the docs to see that many patients, you understand, just *advising* them about the financial facts of life.

Most offices try to pick up the pace by having nurse practitioners or some other resources—videos, Web sites, hand-out sheets—available to help you figure it out on your own. Honestly, most docs don't want to rush, either. We don't get to know you, your child, or your family the way we'd like. Time spent in knowing who you are is the most precious commodity, and many docs put in excess hours for that reason alone. Twelve-hour days for pediatricians are the rule, not the exception. It's easy to blame us for not having time or when something gets missed, but try to trust me on this subject. It's not how we want it, either.

When to Change Your Doctor

A pologies and excuses aside, it's time to consider changing doctors if you're having these problems:

- Miscommunication. The moments you do have with your doctor are precious and few: make sure they count. If he's too distracted or busy to actually hear what you're saying, and he can't do more than spit out a stock answer, he's not doing his job.
- Missed diagnosis more than twice. Anyone's allowed to make *one* boo-boo, but . . .
- Personality mismatch. This applies to the doc, nurse, and/or office staff. Don't put up with unreceptive receptionists.

In these days of megagroup medicine, you may have to choose another doc in the same group to solve your problems. If you do get a sympathetic ear, let him or her know your concerns and complaints about the previous doctor.

TIP

199

Help from EMS-C

EMS-C stands for Emergency Medical Services for Children, and not every suburb or neighborhood has it.

Ambulance services train their medics and paramedics to treat both adults and kids. Since children make up a minority of calls, some of the skills medic classes teach specifically for kids dim with lack of use. Before an emergency strikes, make sure your EMS has pediatric training (or retraining) classes and children-sized equipment and medication doses.

Above all, find out where children are taken in an emergency. Although not all hospitals have pediatric specialists, most situations don't need anything more than a well-trained emergency physician. A hospital with a good reputation for treating kid-emergencies will have a plan in place for situations that call for true pediatric specialty care, including a quick referral line to the children's hospital ER, intensive care unit, or transport team.

TIP

200

Motor Development: Twelve to Eighteen Months

Once your baby begins walking—the definitive requirement for reaching toddlerhood—the developmental journey is not over. Walking takes almost no time to master, and then it's on to running. Forget crawling—he'll never stoop so low again. He's learned a far more efficient means of locomotion. Try to get a couple of good videos of it.

Along with the newfound ability to cover great distances in short order, he'll scale new heights as well: stairs. Going down is more smoothly mastered than going up, but by eighteen to twenty months, he should be pretty good at scrambling up and down.

Fine motor skills take off in early toddlerhood, and have a much longer way to go. These are the hand and individual finger coordination skills that will one day result in handwriting, accurate throwing, and video-game joystick maneuvering. For now, coordination comes down to the simple skills of stacking and holding a crayon steadily enough to scribble on a piece of paper.

TIP

201

Motor Development: Eighteen to Twenty-Four Months

After eighteen months, you'll probably stop paying attention to her gross motor skill development, which is still a work in progress. Jumping and balancing become achievements (as noted by her improvement in reaching the cookie jar and fascination with furniture bouncing). Throwing transforms itself from mere flinging bottles away to quarterback-like finesse.

But fine motor skill acquisition is really where it's at. This is the time for some *useful* skills. She's learning how to wash herself or brush her teeth (lend a hand if you actually want her gums and teeth to benefit), put on clothes, and take them off again in order to put on something else that catches her eye.

She's piecing together puzzles, and has more control using crayons and markers. Drawing, for most toddlers this age, is stalled on scribbling, but the days of copying and making recognizable shapes are coming fast.

TIP

202

Motor Development: Two to Three Years

My, how time flies! By his second birthday, that heady, breathless thrill of watching him take his first step seems a lifetime ago, doesn't it? Now he's on the threshold of sports: throwing a baseball or football, tossing a basketball through a hoop, gymnastics. In the Rockies, kids are on skis by two and a half, and they're pretty good by three!

Fine motor skills also proceed at a magical pace. The first "picture" a child can copy is a circle, followed by a plus sign. By two and a half, a face consisting of several circles and an arc may appear on construction paper. By three, nose-mouth-eyes are joined by ears, hair, and maybe even a body.

Getting clothed is a proud accomplishment by the third birthday, and mastering buttons comes in by the fourth birthday. Of course, don't expect miracles. Scientists are still baffled as to when children actually develop the motor skill of picking up their toys . . .

TIP

Art Project: Origami

A project that takes a greater degree of skill (meaning you do it first and your child watches for the next few times) is the ancient Japanese art of paper folding, origami. Find a book at the local Barnes 'n' Borders or library. Even if she can't make the zendo bird (good luck making it yourself!) she can at least make a cup or swan after a few tries.

Art Project: Glue Masterpiece

Glue. It ain't just Elmer's anymore. Or, rather, it is Elmer's, and a whole lot more. Glue is an entire medium unto itself, ripe for a toddler's imagination.

Coat a sheet of construction paper with glue. Using at least three colors, throw on paper strips and sparkles. Add dried rice and pasta bits. Add some sand, too.

Instant beachscape, complete with gulls (the pasta), foam (rice), and a pretty blue sea (sparkles).

TIP

205

Language Development: Twelve to Eighteen Months

That first magic word! The wonder of that first breathy, repeated syllable that was something besides Ma or Da!

The single precious word is joined by another, and another, and in no time it's a dozen, then two dozen. By about thirty or forty words, she starts linking them together into phrases (which she may interpret as single words): "no want," "thank you," "all done." These achievements represent *expressive* language accomplishments. Her *receptive* language skills are far more advanced than this, however. In other words, she understands far more than she can repeat. For anyone who's tried to learn another language, you know this to be true: it's much easier to understand what's being said than to repeat a phrase or respond in kind.

Thus, at a year and a couple of words, she can understand—and demonstrate comprehension of—single-command tasks like "Point to your belly button" or "Give me the ball."

TIP

206

Language Development: Eighteen to Twenty-Four Months

In the second half of year two, he can be understood, at least some of the time, by folks other than his parents. He'll be able to tell you what he wants in one- or two-word phrases. His vocabulary is at 50 to 100+ words, and growing. He'll start to publicly embarrass you with those cute little private things he repeats.

On the receptive side of the coin, his RECORD is still miles ahead of the REPLAY. He can follow two- and then three-step commands: "Stop what you're doing," "Put that back," and "Come to the table." Whether he actually bothers to carry these out or not is, of course, up for negotiation. But if he *wanted* to, he'd be able to do it.

TIP

207

Garbled Speech: Twelve to Eighteen Months

Opening the door to speech is also the opening for trouble and confusion for many families. If no clear first word emerges by thirteen or fourteen months, the questions start: Is this normal? Is he okay?

About half of all children add a word to Mama or Dada by a year, but it takes up to twenty-one months for 90 percent of children to say more. That's a long time to wait and still be normal—but normal is still possible.

More commonly, there is a mix of clear and unclear speech. Some of this comes from a child making experimental sounds, just playing with what is and is not considered "speech." Other times it's just inexperience. If the majority of words he's trying to say are garbled or unclear, there are two possible problems: the mouth (articulation) or the throat (vocalization). In both cases, questions can be answered by several specialists: developmental-behavioral pediatricians, speech pathologists/therapists, ear-nose-throat surgeons, or neurologists.

Nontalkers

Some children prefer silence. One of the most common variants of normal development is the nontalker. Nontalkers have normal receptive-language skills, as demonstrated by understanding normal speech and instructions. Their hearing is also normal—they hear and register sounds without relying on other senses, such as sight. The child just does not talk, which is not an uncommon situation. Parents excuse this as letting the older kids "do the talking for them" or pass it off as shyness. They are betraying their own lingering concerns that a problem is lurking that the docs just haven't caught yet.

The truth is, however, that many kids who start talking late eventually catch up completely. Their speech is, by age three or four, no different than a child who first recited the Gettysburg Address at eleven months old. Sometimes these children continue to be quiet, even among playmates. They save their filibusters for home and hearth.

A periodic re-evaluation by a speech therapist may be appropriate until the child is speaking on a par with other playmates. If nothing else, the evaluations will reassure you all is well.

Social Development: Twelve to Eighteen Months

The very notion of social development is a mixed bag. Toddlers combine their advancing motor and language skills and test them out in the arena of playmates and parents. Therefore, social development is the emergence of personality with the greater and more complex tools at your child's disposal. A placid, shy child takes these skills and plays happily in new situations and with new companions. An aggressive child hurls himself off furniture and wrecks the toys of any friend he's placed with. Some children leave stranger shyness behind and adapt easily to a world with new adults (teachers and play date parents), while others remain clingy. They'd rather conduct their experiments in separating from Mom and Dad in the privacy of their own family room.

In other words, social development in young toddlers is completely unpredictable, individual, and chaotic. With this exception: they all want a security blanket.

TIP

210

The Tantrum

By the second half of the second year, the direction of all social development points one way and one way only: tantrums.

After about a year and a half, all children get the concept of independence. Once they comprehend that they can choose the food to put in their mouth and the clothes they cover themselves with, the big social experiment they're interested in is which buttons on Mom and Dad can be safely pushed without getting busted.

The tools at their disposal are limited: asking for something or loudly demanding it. They've learned that superior force is sometimes needed to accomplish a goal (you *have* pulled them away from a hot oven, haven't you?). What they haven't learned, and will through a series of tests (a.k.a. tantrums) over the next year or so, is that you can't always get what you want.

TIP

211

Early Toddling: Falls 'n' Bumps

A painful consequence of the first weeks of toddling about on a pair of unsteady legs is a steady succession of bumps and collisions. A one-year-old's eyes, in the first weeks of walking, are aimed on the shelved toy he wants, not on the toy he left on the floor five minutes ago. Plan to take pictures of him walking in a month or two, once all the forehead bruises have faded. In summertime, expect lots of purple, red, and yellow-brown marks on the shins and forearms he acquired from running around in shorts. Ignore the stares of the other parents out there. No, you're not beating your child.

Brush up on the signs indicating a minor vs. significant head injury. Toddler tumbles while walking or running on a flat surface don't usually result in serious head trauma. Keep a supply of Tylenol and cold-packs on hand, in addition to a ready supply of hugs and available lap-time.

TIP

Late Walkers

Slow to walk? She ought to be steady on two feet by thirteen months, but what if month fourteen slips by and she's not? When is a delay a sign of trouble?

Some children are late walkers, and it may be hereditary. Either parent may have been a late walker. (Grandma ought to recall when her baby "finally" walked.)

If at fifteen months he's still not motoring along, it's time to have a developmental assessment. A general delay carries over into other areas, so speech and language milestones may show delays as well.

Neurologic and muscular disorders are sometimes tipped off by not walking. Signs of weakness in other muscle groups are evidenced by difficulty holding a bottle or a weak grip. Feeding difficulties, such as constant choking or gagging are a sign of weakness coordinating the many oropharyngeal (mouth and pharynx) muscles involved in sucking and swallowing.

If, however, the problem is confined to a reluctance to walk independently, take a deep sigh of relief, but make sure you get the question answered by a good, medical evaluation.

TIP

213

Good Shoes

The adorably expensive Weeboks and Baby Nikes or Gymborees that look so cute in formal portraits are *not* meant for walking. Once he's a biped with a purpose, take him to a good children's shoe store. He needs a pair of shoes to support his arch and bear his weight appropriately.

Establish a relationship with the nice man who sizes up teeny tootsies for a living. He'll tell you if the shoes your neighbor passed on to you fit, and if they're sturdy enough for a new set of feet. (Hey, he may even have sold the pair of shoes long ago!)

Your dependence on the shoe man costs a little more, but for the next two or three years, it's worth it. Don't burn your bridges by going into the same store two or three times to "try on" shoes and then leave empty-handed, only to get them at a discount online somewhere. It's not fair to the shoe-store owner trying to make a living, and he won't offer his services to you if you're cheating him. Then, when a nice pair of hand-me-down shoes comes along, you won't have anyone to turn to for a quick check.

TIP

214

Limping

Every toddler experiences a limp or limb pain at some point or another, but it's rarely a symptom of anything serious. There are two important questions that sort things out: fever and trauma. If there's been an injury and no fever, the limp or pain may be from a fracture or slight bruising. A fracture may be only minimally swollen but is persistently painful with marked, localized tenderness. Not a wimpy, vague, "I think it hurts 'cuz you're asking me" kind of hurt.

Combined fever and pain *without* injury represents a possible infection of the bone or joint. Both are serious, but a joint is far more susceptible to immediate damage, so have this checked ASAP.

If there's been no fever and no immediately identifiable injury, check again with your doc. In this situation, a minor fall or tumble somewhere along the way may be recalled, and will often explain the situation.

Growing pains are a separate issue.

TIP

Into the Wild

The very nature of toddling is exploration. It's a continuance of the journey started by crawling, only with a far more efficient means of locomotion. Getting into everything, the quintessence of toddlerhood, is the point. Prepare for it: It's not the exception to the rule, it *is* the rule. Learn along with your child. A familiar toy cabinet or closet is no longer just a place to keep her favorite friends (or her favorite pair of daddy shoes); it's a destination, filled with all sorts of interesting whoozits and whatzits she never really thought of before.

The garage? A cave of wonders. Laundry room? *Terra incognita*. The job of setting limits on what's safe or permissible to explore is distinct from your frustration over things you've told her *not* to do, see, or pick up a thousand times already.

TIP

216

The Diapering Challenge

A ll those times your little darling boy simply lay down and let you change his diaper were, he suddenly realizes, sadly missed opportunities for serious *fun*. For the next few weeks, get ready for his favorite new game of *wisky-WASSSky!*—a charming entertainment consisting of head thrashing and arm flinging while you try to clean the hideous combination of last week's lingering remnants of gastroenteritis plus last night's corn. The more pitching and rolling the better!

Not so easy anymore, is it? After cajoling, pleading, and occasionally threatening, he keeps playing. What can you possibly do to get diapering over with? Try anything that works. For pee-only diapers, have him stand. Distract him with a toy or book and keep him focused on that while you do your handiwork. Put Daddy or Grandma on the phone. No one around? Call the weather service, or anyone with an answering menu. A few years ago, a memorable e-mail directed me to dial an 800 number with the option: *"To hear a duck quack, press 8,"* followed by—yes, a duck quack.

TIP

217

Mommy, Don't Go!

Just as there are children who walk or talk later than the rest, some toddlers cling to the safety of Mom or Dad rather than explore an ever-changing world. This internal struggle, between dependence and independence, can be a tough boundary for some children to cross. Offer a little assistance. Let her know, when you leave, that you'll return at a certain time, showing big and little hands on the clock for assistance. Dedicate some time alone with her, but let her know that when this special play date ends, you have to go out. Shopping, work, international intrigue. Whatever. It's your life.

She'll retreat into the safety and security of her prized blanket, and welcome you, upon your return, not with smiles and joy, but a torrent of tears and complaints. Now that you're back, of course, she can let it all loose.

TIP

218

Mine, Mine, Mine!

As a rule, an important rule, one-year-olds understand nothing of the rights and feelings of others. With their own needs and desires high up on a pedestal, despite a little fuzziness over the distinction between a need and a desire, they yank toys from the hands of their erstwhile playmates.

At first, while they're asserting their wants, you have an opportunity for teaching the law of taking turns. But in time, the selfishness turns into doggedly oppositional behavior. He knows it's wrong, but he doesn't know how wrong it is until he tries it a few times and learns how much trouble he gets into.

This is a long process of change, especially if he's too young to realize that being hit by his friend and suffering a hostile toy takeover are related situations. In other words, reminding him that he didn't like being hit *either* may take a long time to sink in.

Be persistent, be patient. Learning to share and learning to respect the rights of others takes a lifetime. But he'll get it eventually. Just give the process the time it needs and deserves.

TIP

219

Throwing Stuff

One way for little Joey to express delight over a newfound motor skill is to throw any and every object that he can get his chubby little paw halfway around. This poses a far greater hazard to parents of winter babies than summertime babies. If this becomes *the* irresistible game for your child, channel the energy as best you can. Especially if you're cooped up in a long, Syracuse-style winter (snow and subzero temps from Halloween until Easter), clear a zone for fastball practice where he won't damage any family heirlooms. Establish rules for what is and is not his to throw. Carry through on the consequences when he steps outside the lines.

Show him other things that fly: paper planes, Frisbees, boomerangs.

Pray for sunny, warm weather.

TIP

220

Bladder Infections

Urinary tract infections are common in little girls thanks to a short urethra. It's so short that a hardy bacterium can hike all the way up to the bladder, and there it thrives. A thriving bacterium reproduces and reproduces again, and this is known as a bladder infection, or UTI.

The things that allow bacteria to gain a foothold (or pseudopod-hold) include nylon panties or six hours in a bathing suit. A two-year-old who pinches her labia may have germs on her (unwashed) fingertips. A bit of toilet paper or torn diaper-wipe may contain intestinal bacteria that make their way into the urinary system. This is why the intestinal bacterium E. coli is the most common offender in urine cultures.

Signs and symptoms include fever, tummy ache below the belly button, and pain or discomfort during urination. You may notice a little dancy-pants routine—that's the pain and discomfort.

Go to your pediatrician for a urinalysis and culture. If it is, in fact, a UTI, you'll get a prescription for antibiotics.

TIP

Swollen Lymph Nodes

Lymph nodes are all over the body. Most people are familiar with the ones along the neck, but they also have locations inside the mouth (tonsils and adenoids are lymph nodes), the armpit, in front of the ear, the groin, and inside the elbow, to name several. They are frontline protection against infection, and swell up when activated for germ warfare.

This is a good thing. Children under age five are susceptible to a whole host of infections, particularly in wintertime, and therefore it may seem as if they've always got swollen tonsils or nodes along the neck. Relax and remember: they're supposed to.

Occasionally a lymph node loses the battle and becomes infected itself. In such cases, the node is painful and swollen (as happens with strep and mono, but minus the next couple of symptoms). It becomes red, warm, and tender to the touch. This situation requires antibiotics.

In the very unusual case when all the lymph nodes swell at once, get to a doctor: a number of serious illnesses, including leukemia and lymphoma may do this.

TIP

222

Night Watch

Long after the trauma over baby sleep battles recede into the distance like a troubled nightmare of long ago, and just as the assurance of a good night's sleep becomes firmly ingrained as a constitutional right, it comes . . . the next wave.

Most kids wake up once or twice in the night—and promptly go back to sleep. But sometimes this sets the stage for a toddler relapse. Toddlers can get into the habit of waking up and issuing demands—a bottle, a diaper change, a story, a song.

Help him once; help him twice. If, by the third or fourth night in a row, you find the requests escalating, you're headed for trouble. Set a limit on the assistance you're willing to give and then prepare for another few nights of anguished, forlorn cries. It's just a bump in the road. He'll settle back into good sleeping habits soon enough.

TIP

Early Risers

Fear it. Some kids arise at the crack of 5:30 in the morning and no force on earth will change it. This is fine if:

1. You wake up at 0500 anyway for a morning drill
2. The baby is up at 5 A.M., too
3. You come in from work at that hour and this counts as family time
4. All of the above

If, and it's wildly possible, *none* of the above apply to you or any willing member of your household, it is still possible to get some shuteye while he's up and at 'em. Give him a glass of juice and a muffin and set up toys in a play area so he can amuse and feed himself in safety until you're a bit more ready to tackle the world. Then pray that it works.

TIP

224

Sofa-Sized Art

Interior decorators are always on the lookout for new ways to breathe life into a home. What better way to convey the warmth of a home than by deeply expressing one's innermost self?

Save a kitchen or family room wall for the Dada-esque collages of play group. Change the displays with the seasons: the Halloween oeuvre, the Passover celebration. Search your local craft store (or Wal-Mart) for washable markers and easy-off paints. Hang a whiteboard or magnetic board dedicated to little Jimmy and his creations. With any luck, you'll avoid the more personal and pungent forms of self-expression . . .

TIP

Art Project: Sponge Painting

The thing about paintbrushes is that they're so, well, *twentieth century*. Sponges, like food, can be molded or cut into a multitude of shapes for a variety of effects. In fact, the concept can extend to just about any item a toddler can get her paws around, dip into a paint well and apply to paper: feathers, toothbrushes. Why accept limits? Make a game of just searching through the house to see what becomes a paintbrush next.

This is another notion stolen, I confess, from the halls of my daughter's preschool, but one I wish I'd had back in the day.

TIP

226

Art Project: Rubber Stamps

When you've tired of abstracts, it's time for the real world. (Although, like Rome, when you're tired of abstracts, you're tired of life itself.) Any halfway respectable toy store has, in some cheapo back aisle, a set of rubber stamps: animals (real and imaginary), letters, numbers, and shapes.

Create a comic book that tells stories. Let him do the artwork with the rubber stamps, then ask him what each picture means. Or, suggest a story: the family's last visit to Grandma's, his day at the zoo. Using a real outing you've had as a subject, paste photos alongside his artwork—you'll have a real keeper.

TIP

227

Art Project: Cutting Paper

The delirious pleasure of cutting construction paper must be studiously withheld until about age two and a half. Then, with safety scissors and close supervision, let him make cutout designs and projects. No child who's ever tasted the sweet thrill of carving up pumpkin-orange sheets and gluing them to a deep-sea blue background is ever going to be content with less again. Nor will your floor ever be completely free of chips, slivers, and punches of paper.

TIP

228

Persistent Birthmarks

Somewhere between the languid pace of paint drying and the protracted drift of continental plates is the slow crawl of changes in your baby's skin. The first birthday is a good time to take stock of some of those changes. True birthmarks that should have faded are stork bites and Mongolian spots. They may still be noticeable to a discerning, maternal eye, but for the rest of the world they will have vanished.

"Birth" marks such as brown moles (a.k.a. nevi) may have appeared. Bright red or purple raised marks, known as cavernous hemangiomas ought to be fading. A flat hemangioma, known as a port wine stain, may be permanent. These are actually vascular malformations, meaning abnormal beds of capillaries, and the color results from excess blood under the skin.

As recently as the 1980s, many of these marks were considered permanently disfiguring lesions. Newer laser technology can completely eliminate them in many cases. It's slow but removes them without scarring. Ask your friendly neighborhood doctor.

TIP

The TV Turn Rule

When your children get to squabbling like India and Pakistan over whose turn it is to commandeer the TV remote (or Play Station controls or Game Boy), have a permanent rule waiting in the wings: The child born on an odd day gets his turn on odd days. If both are born on an odd day of an even month of an even year, you're not out of luck.

Invoke the *firstborn* then *second-born* lineup.

The Nonstop Runny Nose

A nose running for six weeks and counting can drive any sane mom or dad to psychosis. The evil causes most often feared are allergy, sinusitis, or the dreaded SEW (Something Even Worse) syndrome. They lose sight of a basic truth: most children could care less about their chronically shnuppy noses.

Alas, there is usually nothing more to blame than an extended, undistinguished cold virus. A one-year-old in day care is exposed to germ upon germ, and individual colds run into each other. The natural time-course for a cold is two to three days of cough and congestion, followed by another day or two in which the clear nasal discharge turns yellow or green (as immune cells start striking back in force) and then it's gone. Day care attendees, however, have both phases extended by a week or more. And after a ten- or eleven-day cold, it's time for the next cold to strike.

Certain signs or symptoms should prompt a doctor's visit: inability to eat or drink comfortably due to airway blockage; wheezing; snoring or sleep disturbance; return of high, spiking fevers.

TIP

Choosing Playmates

In baby play groups, you got a chance to watch and coo over the little darlings, and gossip with your friends. But a toddler is different. The dial turns from parallel to *shared* play. *He'll* decide who he likes to play with; you won't necessarily approve.

There is a natural tendency to nit-pick the playmates' behavior: Conor's too aggressive *or* he's going to pick up Ben's habit of whining *or* Sammy yells too much. And opposites certainly attract, even at this age. All of this is guaranteed to make you crazy.

Try to respect his choices. The appropriate intervention is not to set limits on the children he plays with but to temper the ensuing misbehaviors: "Neil shouldn't scream indoors, and you shouldn't, either." "When Zach doesn't share, that's not nice, either."

Work out ahead of time how the other child's parent wants you to respond. And when you drop off your son, make sure the other parent has your blessing to redirect or correct his behaviors when he crosses the line.

TIP

Aggressive Behavior

Oh, little Angelica is a perfect angel! All the other parents say so, too! Reports of her bullying and hitting are just, well . . . jealousy! Hell-o-o? Anyone home? Anyone listening? You won't improve your child's social standing by letting her get away with murder (or assault and "bitery").

A child who behaves in a perfectly acceptable way at home for her parents may be an aggressive hellion to her friends. She may be masking shyness or anxieties with aggressive or combative behavior. Removing the privilege of a play date may resolve the problem, but only temporarily because she doesn't have to face the unwanted social situation. If she's getting carried away while enjoying herself, but not respecting her friends' rights, it *is* appropriate to limit her participation until she's established a little more self-control.

Be fair to the other kids, and the other parents will be fair to you.

TIP

233

Hosting the Play Group

A wonderful way to encourage a two-and-a-half-year-old's sense of independence is to allow her to plan her own party.

Draw up a guest list and help her make the phone calls. Let her propose one or two activities they'll all do. She may come up with a surprise: a kickball game or Let's Make Cupcakes. Once the gang is assembled, she may need a little oversight, but remind her she's in charge of the fun, including conflict resolution. You both might be in for the surprise of your life. (Hopefully the good kind.)

At the end of the party, review with her all the ways in which she rose to the occasion and how proud of her you are. No child ever forgets this kind of praise.

Hitting

Dr. Frankenstein isn't the only one who created a monster. You teach your child to stand up for his rights and insist he have a turn, but if that doesn't work, he may decide the next-best tactic is to pop his best friend right in the kisser.

This is when to trundle out the lesson: "Find an adult if you can't solve the problem. Don't hit." Now that you've invited yourself as a third party to the conflict, you need to show how to negotiate a settlement that doesn't involve clobbering. Let's say the playmate who won't share a toy is also pretty stubborn and won't give up. Put the toy away if neither side will give in, and call off any future play dates if the two can't seem to ever play nicely.

If the problem is aggressiveness in group situations, plan play dates with someone he gets along with one-on-one. In preschool, this may mean some extra maneuvering, but in time he'll come around and behave in a less combative manner.

TIP

235

Breath-Holding Spells

By the time a child can *tell* you he's going to hold his breath until he turns blue, you have little to worry about. But sometime after age nine months, certain kids display the alarming talent of holding their breath.

The medical term is, truly, "breath-holding spell." There are two types: a *blue spell* results when a child exhales and can't restart drawing in the next breath. It may progress to the point where the heart rate falls and the child has a brief (under a minute) seizure. When they lose consciousness, they resume breathing.

The other kind is a *pale spell*, where the heart rate drops after taking a deep inhalation. The child turns pale and seems to go out of it, then recovers.

These spells are brought on by anger and frustration, and are a furious form of tantrum.

If I haven't scared the daylights out of you by now, I'm losing my touch.

Here's the punch line: Children outgrow these spells without any evidence of having done themselves any harm. There's no known medical treatment, but a behavioral therapist may be able to teach you how to avoid triggering such a wave of anger.

TIP

236

Taking Turns

Until the time you ask her to take turns with a toy, she has been the queen bee, the geocentric hub of the universe. Why *should* she? It's *hers!*

A deep-seated, full-throated refusal to take turns doesn't mean selfishness. It just means she's never before considered that something isn't hers. So before she inflicts a temper tantrum on a close playmate, start out by taking turns with her yourself. At around eighteen months, set aside a play date for you and her.

Sometimes you get to serve the tea set first, next time she'll go first. Another useful maneuver: mark her toy-time with "three more minutes" then "one more minute" and then "time to let me have a turn."

It won't happen overnight, or in a week, or even a month. This is a concept to be mastered over the long haul.

TIP

237

Sharing

Sharing is the other half of taking turns.

It means she can't have a toy all to herself when someone else has a claim to it: a visiting friend, the curious baby. (Her blankie is a special exception.) Or, if she has appropriated an item that belongs to you or the family dog, she needs to understand that you or the puppy are "sharing" with her, but the deed to possession has not been transferred.

Like turn-taking, explain sharing to her rationally when she's *not* melting down. There are oceans of setbacks and retreats along the way, such as the lost or broken toy, the grabby friend, the inconsiderate baby brother.

At the end of the day, share your sharing frustrations with your partner over a nice glass of wine. I suggest a Merlot.

The Pre-emptive Strike

Skies darken and the air grows heavy before a thunderstorm. Signs abound, and tuning in to them is no difficult task. So, too, with a two-year-old about to let loose the tempests of Hades.

If a placid play date with his best friend, Jonah, suddenly begins to sound like an episode of Jerry Springer, toys tossed and tempers flaring, start battening down the hatches.

Gently, unobtrusively, place yourself into the activity and gently close it down. Offer to read a book, give a snack, pop in a short video.

Don't give him the chance to erupt in a torrent of anger, cries, and throwing.

Fashion Trends

No self-respecting toddler lets you dress her once she develops her own eye for fashion. Sorry, Mom, but you're outta your mind if you think I'm gonna wear pants and a sweatshirt just because it's freezing outside. It's shorts 'n' short sleeves for me!!!

Such negotiations can really chew up a morning. The Question, the ever-loving, ever-present Question—fight or give in?—is getting kind of old, and you have to get to the doctor appointment.

Don't negotiate when there are no options: let her throw a tantrum, throw a coat over her and go. If, however, there aren't any pressing matters to attend to, and she can play indoors in her shorts, let her have her way.

If she insists on wearing the weirdest of outfits, even in public, don't sweat it. School? No way. Play? Okay. Chances are good that one of her friends also sports the argyle and Miss Piggy look, and they'll have themselves a delicious little giggle fit over that.

TIP

240

Carry Me!

Why should I, your daughter asks herself, *go to the immense trouble of walking when your arms are perfectly suited to carry me? Walking is so five minutes ago!*

She may be melting down, she may be tired, she may just be manipulating you (evidence of the latter is an instantaneous transformation from whiny and helpless to smiley and bouncy). But, like any other tactic, the reasons for the behavior are often easy to identify: she wants attention, reassurance, warmth, or she wants to test you. If your back can stand it, lift her up for a piggy-back ride as your non-negotiable offer. It keeps your arms free for everything else. She may refuse because it's not so snuggly and warm up there, or just for the sake of refusing.

Now it's your call.

TIP
241

The Whiner

Whining is incurable. Just look at your business colleagues, family, friends, people you pass in the mall—they all demonstrate the intractability of whine-itis.

But in the privacy of your own family, you can limit the whine and drone of a toddler. The most successful tactic is to tackle it head on: "You're asking in a whiny voice. That hurts my ears. I'll give you a bottle when you ask nicely." When this is met by an even higher-pitch "Noo-o-o-o-o!" or "I can't sto-o-o-op!" turn your back and ignore it. Give her a couple of chances, and you should get a calmer, but sniffly, request minus the whining.

Sometimes it's wise to let a little whininess run its course, especially if she's tired and trying to entertain herself. In a play group or other social situation, let her know when she's speaking in an unacceptable voice, and restate for her, nicely, what it is she wants. This takes time and patience. And you can't expect to get anywhere if you're whining yourself.

TIP

242

Two-Year-Old Toy: Sorting

A two-year-old can be very particular. The ducks go *here*, the penguins *there!* This can hold for just about every aspect of their life except when it comes to putting all the Legos back where they belong or getting all her doll clothes back into the dresser.

Toys created with sorting in mind are soft (cloth) briefcases with multiple pockets, and shapes in each pocket. You can find them for numbers and alphabets, Noah's Ark, months, and weekdays.

TIP

243

Two-Year-Old Toy: Jigsaw Puzzles

For precocious puzzle connoisseurs who have left the eight-to-ten-piece wood puzzles behind, move up to jigsaw puzzles. Up to fifty pieces offer a doable challenge (with little or no help) and hold her attention for at least ten minutes. Do a series of five or six puzzles, and save them to show Dad when he comes home at the end of the day.

Ravensberger puzzles are particularly high quality in artistry and construction. They travel well from one family to the next (as hand-me-downs)—as long as you can keep all the pieces together, that is.

TIP

244

Two-Year-Old Toy: Railroad Tracks

Budding architects or engineers show their hand early. The perfect birthday or holiday present is a big set of wooden train tracks that can be designed and redesigned in countless variations. Take a picture of him sitting in the middle of his bigger accomplishments. Because you can always add special pieces—crossings, bridges, landscaping—the sets solve the eternal Grandma problem of "What does he want that he doesn't already have?"

Even after he turns his attention to other toys for weeks at a time, he'll always come back to it on his own or when a friend comes over for a play date.

TIP

245

Two-Year-Old Toy: Waterworks

The same set of skills that are drawn on to assemble railroad tracks are used to build an aqueduct. And it's the same kind of fun—only splashier. Brio makes an interlocking waterway set complete with boats, bridges, locks and docks. It's a great outdoor toy in summer.

A more vertical version of the build-it-and-they'll-have-fun principle is a marble maze. Interlocking hollow tubes and cylinders fit together to let a marble follow a trail through steps and swirls. Your two-year-old will probably let you help build it, and then hog all the marble dropping himself. Beware roving pretoddlers, however, who will look on it as delightfully smashable.

TIP

246

Two-Year-Old Toy: Kitchen Set

On the costly-but-worth-it scale, the best bang for your toy buck is an elaborate, fully stocked PlaySkool or LittleTikes kitchen set. Save it for "winter holiday gift season" (to be perfectly nondenominational) or a birthday and remember to save the box to use as a new puppet theater.

When you wake up in the morning, ask your child to make you breakfast. Start with some soup, milk, or coffee. Make a very, very big deal about it not tasting very good. Screw up your face in intense concentration as you finally determine that what's missing is that it "needs some giraffe!"

Return the cup for her to add giraffe, then take a teensy sip when she hands it back. It can taste perfectly fine (accompanied by a big "*aaaah!*") or it may be horrible and yucky, in which case spit it out noisily (*dryly*, to avoid imitators) and tell her it's got too much concrete in it. Dispense big hugs and kisses when it finally tastes just right.

The best sign that this is a great game: "Again, again soup!"

TIP

247

Two-Year-Old Toy: Sticker Storybooks

Not only are sticker books cheap and disposable, they can be easily stored away in a diaper bag. Always have one on hand for unexpected delays: at the doctor's office, in traffic on the way to Uncle Jamie's, waiting for the food to appear at an unexpectedly busy restaurant.

Just as folks who fly on a regular basis know to always have a toothbrush in their carry-on bag, savvy parents will tell you this is a basic item for predictable emergencies.

TIP

248

Two-Year-Old Toy: Tea Set

Copying Mommy? Controlling his own world? Letting his somewhat unanchored imagination run wild? Whatever!

Give a two-year-old a tea set and watch an operetta unfold. Boy or girl, anyone can host a party. Along with the tea set, you'll need a small, LittleTykes table and appropriate-sized chairs. And your child will surely supply the stuffed animals. Precious moments like this cry out to be taped and recorded for the Time Capsule. As he serves tea, cake, and cookies to his favorite imaginary playmates, he'll supply stream-of-consciousness dialogue at its pure best.

TIP

249

Croup Care

Croup, a harsh barking cough with sudden difficulty breathing, is a standard-issue childhood illness. It lasts three days and often strikes about an hour after going to bed: children wake up agitated, coughing, and gasping for breath.

In the fifteen-minute trip to the ER, your tyke miraculously starts getting better. By the time I see him at 1 A.M., he's mostly better and the parents are a little sheepish in describing how bad the episode was.

A virus causes the tissue in the throat to swell up, and the chill, dry night air helps it constrict once again. I'll offer medication (an aerosolized version of adrenaline and then steroids) to do the same thing on a more lasting basis. When the coughing resumes back at home, have a cool mist humidifier by the bed. If this doesn't work, go to the bathroom and turn the shower on hot. The warm mist ought to help and if, by gummy, it *doesn't,* then go for a ride in the car and pretend you're the ambulance heading to the ER.

TIP

Give Tylenol or Motrin for fever, and don't ask me, or any doctor, for antibiotics. You'll have a calm night of sleep in another three or four days.

Hives

Hives are big, blotchy, itchy red spots that signal an immediate allergic reaction. Unfortunately, most of the time, it's almost impossible to identify the allergen. As a rule, the common triggers are foods, such as peanuts, eggs, tomatoes, or shellfish; medications; or exposure to environmental agents such as pet hair or bee stings. A simple bout of hives may come and go over hours, but sometimes it lingers as long as two days.

Signs of a more severe allergic response include swelling of the face (lips, throat, eyes, ears), difficulty breathing, nausea, vomiting, and diarrhea. Treatment of a mild case of hives is easy: antihistamines. The same histamine that causes runny noses in a cold also produces this skin flare-up.

For some reason, though, antihistamines, which are of limited effect for a cold, work quite well at busting hives. You can repeat the dose every six to eight hours. If wheezing, stridor, or mouth/throat swelling develop, call 911 or go straight to the closest ER. I'll guarantee they won't make you wait.

TIP

Seizures from Fever

A febrile seizure is a brief episode in which a mommy or daddy witnessing the event suffers more than the child. It is a condition where the sudden body-temperature rise (often to 104 or 105° F) triggers a generalized stiffening, turning blue, eyes rolling to one side. It is followed (in less than a minute) by rhythmic shaking of both arms and legs for five to ten minutes. Afterward the child sleeps for another five to ten minutes, during which time the color should return to normal.

Seizers occur most commonly between the ages of ten months and four years—the first seizure will typically occur between fifteen and twenty-four months. Children outgrow them by age five and have no subsequent risk of developing epilepsy. Simple infections, such as an ear infection or a urinary tract infection, can set off the fever that triggers the seizure. The seizure itself causes no brain damage—except to the horrified parent who is watching at the time.

TIP

Even though the odds indicate that everything will be okay once the episode is over, you should call 911 if your child has never had a seizure before.

252

Vision Problems

Concerns over visual problems usually prove unwarranted under about the age of five. Routine vision screening during healthy-child checks begin in the newborn nursery, so it's rare for problems to go undetected for long.

Myths are hard to break and even harder to disabuse Grandpa of, but sitting too close to the TV doesn't cause eye problems, nor does reading "too much."

The biggest tip-off to disorders such as nearsightedness or astigmatism is squinting or head-tilting to focus on a far-off object. Just to keep terms straight, nearsightedness means the ability to see things that are near and inability to see faraway objects. It's far more common than farsightedness. Astigmatism is distortion of objects near or far, and is caused by a nonspherical cornea. If your child appears to be having difficulty seeing, have his eyes checked. At most, he may need to start wearing glasses at an early age.

TIP

253

Hearing Problem?

Unfortunately, hearing problems and deafness are not as uncommon as vision problems. In many cases, astute parents usually sense a problem early on, even from birth, under the right circumstances. Babies who seem slow to pick up early speech skills are usually correctly diagnosed in the second half of the first year.

But in cases of partial or acquired deafness (from constant, severe ear infections) the diagnosis may not be made until toddlerhood.

Usually, speech difficulties or delays tip off presence of a hearing disorder. Garbled or poorly modulated speech is a sign of faulty auditory input.

Other signs *sound* subjective, but are real enough. Consistent inattention to a parent who's not in his face or lack of response to music are clear indicators of a problem. Diagnostic tests are relatively easy to set up and interpret, and hearing therapy remains one of the few untrammeled rights of health care.

Pneumonia and Bronchitis

The lung is designed much like a tree: the trachea is the main trunk, the bronchi and bronchioles are progressively tapering limbs, and the air sacs that exchange oxygen and CO_2, alveoli, are the leaves. In pneumonia, infection fills alveoli with germs, white blood cells, and fluid. In bronchitis, the air sacs are okay, but the bronchi and bronchioles are involved.

Both start with fever and cough, and gradually both develop a moderate degree of breathing difficulty: a rapid rate of breathing and rib retractions. Bronchitis causes wheezing, while pneumonia does so less often. Distinguishing between the two can be tough without an X-ray.

Bronchitis is viral more often than pneumonia, but in most cases antibiotics are a good way to start. Have a humidifier available, push the fluids, and count on big-time droopiness. Children lack energy when they're this sick, but it all comes back in a few days.

Avoid cough medicines with dextromethorphan or codeine, because a good cough helps to expel the nasty junk and resolves the illness much faster.

TIP

255

Colds and Sinusitis

Scores upon scores of viruses circulate every winter (there is a handful fewer the other seasons) and produce cold upon cold. As soon as one ends, the next kicks in. It's been found in medical surveys that children in day care stay sick with the same cold longer than those not in the general circulation of day care.

Here's where it gets tricky. A sinus infection is a cold that extends into facial sinus cavities, characterized by fever, cough, and *excessive* nasal congestion. The same germs that cause colds cause sinus infections. When the inflamed, swollen sinus cavity becomes secondarily infected with bacteria, antibiotics are brought to the rescue. It's hard for doctors and researchers to agree on what symptoms constitute a sinus infection (as opposed to a cold).

Here's my solution: *always* assume antibiotics won't work. Place a humidifier by the crib or bed, stay away from decongestant and antihistamine medications (unless you want her to sleep), and keep lots of tissue boxes handy.

Head for the doctor when fevers return after the first day or two of illness, or dehydration from vomiting and poor intake are present.

TIP

256

Growing Pains: Real Ones

Growing pains are of murky origin, but are not too hard to recognize. It's almost always a deep thigh pain, often occurring in both legs. It is mostly seen in children ages four to ten, but it can start earlier. The pain occurs in the late afternoon or evening and is clearly *not* a joint pain. No fever, no history of injury. The pains may occur on several evenings each week, and the whole crummy situation can last for months to two years. If the pain lasts all day or wakes your child from sleep, it's time to suspect another problem.

We don't know what causes it, because it leaves no clues: blood tests, MRIs, CT scans, and ultrasounds are all negative. Growing pains represent, therefore, a diagnosis "of exclusion": once we've excluded everything else, we have to give the pain *some* name, and this is the name we give.

What helps? Heat, massage, ibuprofen or Tylenol, and understanding. Once you've established that it's just growing pains, that *should* take some of the sting out of it.

TIP

Night Terrors

A two- or three-year-old child who awakens from sleep in the dead of night shrieking and screaming in fear has night terrors. This goes on for many nights at a time. The oddest thing is that the child falls back asleep afterward and in the morning has no recollection of the previous night's pandemonium.

They are terrors to the parent every bit as much as to the child himself. While it's a common event in two- to three-year-olds, moms or dads torture themselves with fears of terrible pathologies such as a stroke or brain tumor or a behavioral-psychiatric condition such as autism—even after the pediatrician's glib reassurance that it's a benign, well-known condition. Easy for us to say.

TIP

258

Nightmares

A nightmare is a bad, scary dream: oversized monsters, helplessness, situations unbounded by rules of logic or sense. Children develop nightmares as early as a year and a half. They are wholly different from night terrors: children wake up crying and upset, not screaming and in a half-sleep. They'll tell you what happened both at the moment when they wake and again the following morning.

There's a bigger difference between nightmares and night terrors than just recall of the bad dream. The boundaries between reality and fantasy in toddlers are loose to begin with. At a very young age, they may not understand that a dream is just not real, and so their fear is touching and heartbreaking.

Occasional nightmares are the rule rather than the exception. Should your child be experiencing nightmares on a regular basis, it is worth your while to discuss the situation with your doctor. Testing by a child psychiatrist may uncover undue stresses or anxieties that you can then work to eliminate.

TIP

259

Causes of Hair Loss

Babies lose their hair—okay. Toddlers also lose their hair—not okay. A few conditions lead to hair loss:

- Alopecia areata: Patchy hair loss, occurring in clumps. In most cases it begins to grow back after a week or two. If not, topical or oral steroids cool down the scalp inflammation responsible for the hair loss.
- Ringworm: A single or isolated few patches of hair loss that gradually expand. The scalp usually looks red, swollen, and infected. An oral antifungal medication is needed.
- Telogen effluvium: Interruption of the normal hair growth cycle after a febrile illness. Large portions of hair spontaneously fall out. The hair follicles do not become inflamed. Hair growth usually resumes normally in a few weeks.
- Hair pulling: This comes in two forms: braiding and nervousness. In either case, the excess traction on hair follicles causes it to fall out, but steroids aren't the answer.

TIP

260

Nursemaid's Elbow

A condition wholly unique to toddlers is an orthopedic problem known as Nursemaid's Elbow. It is a minor dislocation, or subluxation of the head of the radius, one of the long forearm bones. Feel along your forearm from your pinky to the elbow. You've just traced the ulna, the *other* forearm bone. The radius runs parallel, starting at the thumb, and the portion shaped like a nail head fits into a groove along the side of the ulna. It can pop out of this shallow joint when he falls or is yanked out of danger abruptly (by nannies or nursemaids).

An arm with nursemaid's elbow is held limply at the hip; he won't raise it above the belly button, and is quietly tearful if you urge him to try. There is no swelling or bruising. Oddly enough, children often point to the shoulder or wrist as the site of pain, which is called "referred pain."

A simple maneuver sets it back to normal: flexing the elbow and turning the wrist so the thumb swings outward. But don't try this at home. Go to your pediatrician who has seen this a dozen (or thousand) times before.

TIP

261

Stridor: Shrieky Breath

A symptom that is never a false alarm is stridor, a high-pitched, shrieky breath sound indicating a partially obstructed airway. A completely blocked airway, by contrast, does not permit any airflow in or out, and so is completely *silent*. The causes of stridor are:

- Croup: A viral infection causing tracheal swelling, a barky cough, and fever. It is treated with inhaled epinephrine and a steroid shot.
- Foreign body aspiration: A small toy or toy part accidentally drops into the throat. There is usually a great deal of coughing and distress. The object may descend further into the lung, which immediately improves the situation—but still requires definitive treatment.
- Asthma: A severe attack is accompanied by stridor as well as wheezing.
- Anaphylaxis: Your child may be having a severe and immediate allergic reaction—to peanuts, egg, or some other substance.

TIP

All children with stridor should be taken to an ER, probably by ambulance.

Degrees of Fever

Fever is the mother of all symptoms. Just about every common illness produces a fever sooner or later. Usually sooner. Here's what I know about fever:

- Under a temp of about 106° F, the *fever* does not cause harm, it's the *disease* causing fever. At 105° F or more, there are several serious causes of fever.
- Under 105° F or 106° F, the worst that can happen is a febrile seizure. This is scary, but a typical seizure, lasting five to ten minutes, will not harm your child.
- Under 104° F? Fuggeddabouddit. Any self-respecting virus can raise a child's temp to 104° F. It's not particularly high, it's not dangerous, and by the time your child hits age three, it's a minor miracle if he's never had one.

Any other symptom associated with the fever, like cough, diarrhea, or a rash, is a clue to the true illness.

TIP

263

Kinds of Coughs

Coughing is wonderfully complex—your body designed the cough to rid itself of unwanted mucus, germs, or irritants or to signal a mommy that baby may be in danger. Cough, therefore, is a *sign* of the enemy. A cough compendium:

- Coughs due to simple colds are accompanied by sneezing, congestion, and fever.
- Croup causes a distinctly "barky" cough, predominantly at night.
- Wheezing brings on a high-pitched, sharp cough, with wheezing and rib retractions.
- Allergic coughs tend to run all day, disappearing at night, unlike asthma, which worsens in the wee hours.
- A mild, mucousy cough becoming harsh and juicy and accompanied by higher fevers indicates pneumonia or bronchitis.
- "Whooping" cough, a staccato persistent cough followed by a deep *whoop* from the next, overdue breath is rare, since the advent of the Pertussis vaccine.
- A sudden, distressed cough accompanied by shrieks of air means the child is choking.

Pink Eye

The vast majority of causes for pink eye are pretty benign, no matter how grungy it looks. If both eyes are pink, conjunctivitis or allergy is the diagnosis in over 90 percent of cases. Conjunctivitis is an infection of the conjunctiva, which covers the white of the eye and eyelids. A diffuse, soft pink color without much discharge is almost always of viral origin, often accompanied by fever, runny nose, and headache. A bright red, cobblestone eye with a yucky, thick yellow or green discharge is more likely to be bacterial.

If only one eye is pink, think micro trauma from a floating hair or airborne debris. A slightly more macro trauma is a corneal abrasion or scratch. This is markedly painful, so you won't even see your little guy's red eye, because it'll spasm shut. This is the only condition requiring immediate assistance: a doctor can put in an anesthetic drop, an antibiotic ointment, and cover it with a patch. Abrasions heal completely within twenty-four hours.

TIP

Slip-Ups in Toilet Training 1

"It was just an *acc*ident!"

This means one of two things, and thing two is making in his pants. A poop is embarrassing and stressful. It's pretty common after a new baby arrives, as well as myriad other situations: new play routines, a new way of acting out, a gastrointestinal (GI) bug. Sometimes it indicates a significant degree of constipation. The term "encopresis" is used for children who withhold stool for so long that the colon dilates and doesn't recognize how full it is. This calls for a behaviorist and/or GI specialist.

But for the most part, an accident is an accident. He'll be grossed out enough by the situation to avoid letting it turn into a habit. To be on the safe side, don't scold. Remind him of how far he's come since he was in diapers and that he *almost* always knows how to go on his own.

Slip-Ups in Toilet Training 2

Girls, more than boys, have *wet* accidents. The urethra is so short that the little squirt of excitement at a birthday party, a play date, a funny situation on a video, can dampen those proudly worn panties. Just as you have to keep your cool in a poopy accident, it's no use expressing annoyance. Change her clothes and get on with it. When it gets to be a predictable phenomenon, put the onus on her to *go* before she goes. If, out of the blue, she wets herself several times a day, think medical: a urinary tract infection or, more seriously, diabetes.

Alternatively, think intake: If she's drinking caffeine-rich sodas or high citrus juices she may be experiencing a diuretic effect, which draws water through her kidneys and creates copious, dilute urine.

If her vagina itches and is red, it may be vaginitis, a superficial irritation.

Nutrition: Carbs

Carbohydrates are a complex subject, but I'll try to keep it simple. Simple carbs—glucose, fructose, and sucrose—are as vital as tobacco for your child's nutrition. In other words, none need apply. Frosted cereal, candy, honey, soda are available everywhere and mindlessly cheap. After you've pitched the long, successful battle to control what goes in during babyhood, here come friends and parties, cupcakes and cookies—the works. Simple carbs are immediately available as energy from the digestive tract. If unused, they turn, rapidly, to fat. Permanent, unsightly blubber.

By contrast, complex carbohydrates—breads, rice, spaghetti, cereals—are digested slowly, and release sugar to the bloodstream at a measured pace. Nor do they transform into fat as readily. They are high in fiber, good in the long run for his heart, cancer prevention, and good eating habits. Go for whole-grain bread over white when possible.

It's not as hard as you imagine. Kids can develop a taste for food that's not criminally sweet.

TIP

Nutrition: Protein

Picture this: Proteins build machines for which carbs are fuel. Organs are constructed from tissues, the building blocks of tissues are amino acids. Proteins we eat are digested and deconstructed into amino acids and then reconstructed into our tissues. Very efficient.

It's easy to get four servings a day for all a toddler's needs. Just pick from the following: a cup of yogurt, cheese slices, egg (one whole or two whites), tofu (indistinguishable from ice cream to the fourteen-month-old palate), peanut butter, tuna fish.

Voilà! A diet even a vegetarian family can do. And this is before you add protein-enriched, high-fiber carbs such as whole-grain bread.

TIP

269

Nutrition: Fat

A large chunk of body machinery is composed of fat. Physiologically, it's more efficient to import fat than to manufacture it, so your child's growth actually benefits from a certain amount of fat in the diet. They're not like adults who need to worry about fitting into dresses or their old college jeans.

Do include whole milk (until age two), vegetable oils, and cheese. Highly monounsaturated fats and polyunsaturated fats are better building blocks than hydrogenated, saturated fats such as butter, shortening, or animal fats.

It's all too easy, sadly, to make a kid overweight. Too many sweets and simple carbs elbow their way into their diet. Too many burgers or chicken fingers swamp your child's calorie intake with bad fats and cholesterol, too.

Think Zen. Slow down, and try to trim out fast food.

TIP

270

Nutrition: Minerals

To continue the building analogy: Minerals in your child's diet provide the bolts and welds that keep everything together. Iron is mainly used to produce blood cells; calcium is for bones. Lots and lots of other chemical elements are needed, but I can't get into all of them. Iodine, for instance, is crucial for thyroid hormone; fluoride builds teeth; manganese is a component of the enzymes that process sugar and other nutrients.

You get the picture. A little dab'll do you. By eating a variety of fruits and vegetables, your child recycles the needed minerals from plants and animals that also rely on them. Your child's intestine will delight when it sees a little molybdenum pass by! "Ooh, goody!" it's been known to say. "Just what I had a hankerin' for!"

A little more effort is needed to provide all the minerals required in higher amounts like calcium and iron.

Iron is supplemented in cereal and soybeans. Since it is absorbed much more easily in the presence of vitamin C, a good bowl of cereal and milk takes care of most of a day's needs. Whole grains and beef also provide iron. Calcium is readily available in milk, tofu, and hard cheese.

TIP

Nutrition: Vitamins

Vitamins are complex molecules our bodies need that Mother Nature forgot to give us instructions for. An inefficient design, but there's no point arguing with *me*.

There are two types:

1. Water-soluble B-complex and C vitamins aid in breaking sugars down for use as energy, and building sugar and protein supplies for use when needed.

2. The fat-soluble vitamins, A, D, E, and K:
   - Vitamin D is the central control unit of calcium. It's the one vitamin the toddler needn't eat. Skin produces the vitamin *only* upon exposure to direct sunlight.
   - Vitamin E is an antioxidant that comes in handy in a variety of metabolic processes.
   - Vitamin K helps form blood-clotting proteins.
   - Vitamin A forms light-sensing components in vision cells.

TIP

Instant Blow-Dryer

Here's the situation: After rushing out to get to Jenny's birthday party with no time to spare, your Sophie manages to work off the lid of her juice bottle, getting her dress all wet. No time to turn around, and traffic is hemming you in on all sides.

The solution: Pull over and have her take the dress off. Drape it over the armrest or center console. Shut the side panels so that the hot air coming from the center panel is the equivalent of a hair dryer. Then, buckled in safely again, turn the heater vent on full blast. The dress will be toasty and warm by the time you get to the ball.

College Tuition Someday?

Ever-changing as the e-business world may be, here's one Web site worth a shot. Upromise.com sets up an air miles program for college tuition. Once you enroll and register your credit card, a small chunk of each purchase gets put into a 529 tax-deferred education account.

Shop with its online corporate partners (Borders, Land's End, and others) and a few more pennies are racked up. It adds up over fifteen years, and it's painless besides. It may not pay for the whole shebang but, for my (virtual) money, it's the best offer going.

TIP

274

The Favorite Song: Over and Over . . .

There was a time, though you may recall it dimly, when you saw *The Little Mermaid* for the first time, and you thrilled to the big song-and-dance number, "Under the Sea." Ten thousand repetitions later, you may be ready to go into anaphylactic shock when you hear *"undaah-da-seeee."* And yet, your child is content to listen to nothing else all the way from Milwaukee to St. Paul.

Cool your jets, you can cope.

First of all, don't automatically hit the REPLAY button. She can take turns listening to daddy music and big brother music, and then it'll be her turn again. Second, unless there's a severe national battery shortage, she can listen to it till she graduates from college if she wants—on her own headphone set. Third and finally: one day you'll wish it were still Disney. The teenybop music she'll swoon for when she's nine will all sound the same to you, and she'll look at you like you're some sort of lower order crustacean for not recognizing Britney's new song!

TIP

Kindness Counts

Visit the home-bound elderly. Volunteer at a hospital. Bring ignored, unused baby toys to a shelter.

Charity does begin at home, and it should be a family activity. When he's old enough to understand that he can help, too, have him pick a toy or game he can do without, and let him donate it to the hospital. When disaster strikes—an earthquake, flood, or fire—the supplies most urgently needed are food, clothes, and blankets. Rummage through your possessions for items that can be dispensed with. And even if it gives you a few pangs to give away last birthday's sweater or the Christmas present he still wears—well, that's what charity is really about.

The gift of an old, ugly, discarded outfit is certainly appreciated if it means the difference between being warm and dry or cold and wet. But the truer act of charity arises from giving when giving isn't easy.

TIP

276

Make a Volcano!

A simple science project that places you in approximately the awestruck position of miracle worker (for about a day, which is good enough, anyway) is creating a home volcano.

Measure out a few tablespoons of baking soda (sodium bicarbonate) and place on a dish. By the way, do this outdoors—in a park or on the deck.

Place the dish on an overturned bowl or empty planter, so the "lava" has someplace to flow. Next, measure out a couple of ounces of vinegar (acetic acid) and toss in a few drops of red food coloring to make it look like molten rock. Wearing safety glasses, and keeping the kids back a few steps, pour the vinegar through a funnel attached to a length of flexible, plastic tubing (appropriated from one of your kids' unused toys) onto the baking soda and *poof!* Rumbling, bubbling lava!

Feed the Birdies

Here's a nature project for you and your toddler, who probably already has an interest in our feathered friends.

Buy a bird feeder and seed from a pet store or general supply store. Pick out a tree branch he can watch from the breakfast table or his bedroom—someplace where he can keep an eye on things during the course of his day.

It takes a week or so for birds to register the new eatery and place it in their flight paths, but after that you'll have yourself a new set of household companions.

Follow their doings closely with a good set of binoculars and you'll soon identify your regular visitors, even whole families. They go through the feed surprisingly quickly, and hang the feeder low enough off the branch to deter the squirrels.

A downside: droppings.

TIP

278

No, Now!

Migraine-prone parents will tell you that the most reliable trigger for a real brain crusher is the piercing half-shriek, half-whine of "Wannit *no-o-o-o-o-ow!*"

Instant gratification. On the one hand, it's a natural instinct. The eye-taste coordination registers the ice-cream display and becomes fine whine without a moment's delay. If "not now" means "maybe later," you can deal with it by aggressively refocusing her attention from the goodies to you: "If you listen nicely from now until lunch you can have some," or "If you use an indoor voice my 'no' may turn to 'yes.'"

If, however, no is going to stay no, be clear and firm: "You can't always get what you want." Or "We don't have money for that right now" or "That's a game for older boys" or "We just had lunch, so we're not going to McDonald's now."

TIP

279

Biting and Grabbing

A very interesting phenomenon occurs when your thirteen-month-old's grasping hand (motored about on a fascinating transportation device known as feet) gets a clump of Mommy's hair. Mommy shouts in pain and doesn't seem to like it. Funny, same thing happened when she grabbed baby's hair. Does everyone shout like that?

What starts out as experiment quickly turns to aggression, if she dredges up the memory when unhappy, frustrated, or angry—for whatever reason.

Biting, too, starts out innocently enough, but the consequences are equally painful and damaging. For either behavior, a zero-tolerance approach is the right thing to do. Mete out automatic time-outs. She'll get tired of being grounded pretty quickly, and she'll move on to other fascinations.

TIP

280

The Little Home Wrecker

Every child baptizes his family in the deep, spiritual waters of the fundamental differences between babies and toddlers. Babies stay put and are cute. Toddlers cause nuclear devastation. Even without inflicting physical or emotional torture, every toddler finds, at some time or other, a phenomenally expensive way to leave his mark on his household surroundings. Breaking a treasured antique. Shredding a precious old photo. Ruining the walls with a screwdriver or permanent magic marker. They move quickly: broad swaths of territory can be covered in a heartbeat.

Mom's wails and sobs, and his lengthy, heated discussion with Dad—these are often enough to teach a toddler the permanent lesson that this was *way* past the limits. That he vows to *never, ever* do it again is really beside the point.

He'll hear about it at every future family gathering, including his own lasting landmarks: graduation, wedding, and the birth of his children. Don't think it won't happen just because it hasn't happened yet.

TIP

Teaching Sports

An automatic benefit of parenthood is being granted an aura of perfection—for the first several years, anyway. Global assessment of worthiness aside, you *are*, in fact, a pinnacle of some skill or virtue that you can pass along.

An ideal medium for instilling values and goals is your favorite sport. Succeeding at any sport takes time, practice, and, above all, patience. Never been a hoops hotshot? Start now. Your kid will think you're MJ even if you've never sunk a basket in your life. Are you only a so-so hitter? Who cares! Daughter or son, they can watch in amazement and adoration as you flip the ball upward, *swing*, crack the bat, and send the ball heavenward.

Set no limits on your expectations and you'll find no end to the accomplishments and pride they give in return.

Picnic Time

What makes for a successful picnic are the basics: a quiet, peaceful park; a choice playmate or two; a boathouse; and a breeze. A fourteen- or fifteen-month-old ought to be able to withstand the pitches of a paddleboat on a quiet lake (and she'll look totally adorable in a big, bulky life jacket).

Or bring the bike and trailer along for a ride away from the traffic. In both cases, the key is to keep moving so the flies don't know where to land. A canoe trip in a local stream is also a nice lazy way to while away an afternoon: count the turtles sunning themselves on the logs.

TIP

283

When Mommy and Daddy Go Bye-Bye

The agonizing dilemma of when to leave your precious baby in a babysitter's care for an evening happened the first time at—what? Five months old? Three months for your second child? Now, with a toddler, you're ready for an overnight getaway. So is he.

Scratch that. You are *more* than ready for an overnight getaway. Spend a night at a hotel downtown and take in a live jazz band. Spend a night at the opera. Go bowling. Whatever.

The overnight babysitter should be a trusted neighbor or mom of a play date pal. Check in at bedtime to offer a semblance of the usual nighttime ritual. And promise him a present when you get home in the morning. The present, in fact, is the key ingredient in calming any qualms he may have about your leaving.

One or two successful outings like this and you're ready for a weekend trip! Weekend resort packages are available and affordable, and the daiquiris are chilling now . . .

The Climbing Instinct

Why does your toddler stack boxes and footstools to get to the upper shelves in the family room? For the same reason climbers dream of tackling Everest: Because it's there.

Climbing is instinctual, and a valuable motor skill. In general, it is better to allow climbing under supervision than prohibit it because you're afraid he'll climb himself into a dangerous predicament one day when you're not around.

Here's where your relationship becomes cat and mouse. Get down on your knees in his play area searching for any object that can be stacked for climbing, and then either take it away or remove the upper-level hazards that can topple or spill. He will then creatively find a way to build an ad hoc staircase, and you'll reinspect and take away even more stuff.

Look at the bright side: This encourages motor skills *and* creativity—a two-fer!

TIP

285

Art Project: Celery Painting

When *I* was a kid, vegetables were for eating. Well, to be totally honest, they were for sitting on the plate and not eating. Kids today actually seem to like their vegetables, even if they're still not eating them. A celery stalk makes a cool paintbrush: it makes perfect trees with one end, and moons or smileys with the others.

Another idea: Sculpture. Dip the crudités into paint and air dry. With a good sense of color and shape—carrots are arrows, broccoli is a star-filled sky, cauliflower heads are clouds—you've made a still life in primary colors.

TIP

286

Art Project: Mobile

An advanced degree in construction paper and scissors techniques opens the world of 3-D projects. Take several choice shapes carved from construction paper, punch a hole in each one and reinforce it with tape; then, string them up on wire hangers you've bent into new shapes.

Check out the works of Alexander Calder online, or refer to your local library's collection of art books: Matisse, Renoir, Picasso. Imitation is the sincerest form of flattery, so see what your child can recreate. It's not hard to create something genuinely pretty when you make a mobile, and mobiles make great gifts for Grandpa or a new baby.

TIP

287

Art Project: Windsock

Beauty awaits you in found objects. Something as simple as a paper or Styrofoam cup becomes a morning's activity with a little imagination. Cut out the bottom, paint, marker, or rubber-stamp the outside. Tape a few strips of crepe paper to the tapered end. Poke a hole for string to suspend it. Voilà: windsock.

Once she knows the basics and can make these herself, they make great presents for a trip to a friend or relative's house. Making them can even buy you at least a few minutes to get ready for said excursion.

Imaginary Friends

An imaginary playmate is a normal, dependable developmental milestone. The perfect friend: *Jujube* spilled the milk, not me! If your true-life daughter wants to play mom, who better to rule and punish? And, when your errand running becomes a little too real or a little too jostley, who better to tune out with than good old Jujubes?

Her ethereal companion allows her to work through each day's heavy tasks: responsibility, discipline, consequences. These matters are internalized with the assistance of a readily available, constant companion. Someone, moreover, who speaks the same language she does. Keep her special friend in check, though. Don't include Jujube in games until your child insists she's there. Don't appropriate Jujube to get your child to dress or get into a bath. Children are confused enough without making them wonder if you see fantasy creatures, too.

Hydrophobia: Water Fears

The scientific name for sudden avoidance of water is hydrophobia. Suddenly freaking out at the prospect of taking a bath is just one of those toddler fears that turn up mysteriously after the first birthday.

It may not be the water itself—it may be the noise from the faucet. Or it may be water immersion. Like a fear of dogs, loud noises, or the dark, it's a phase he'll go through for a spell.

How to keep him clean in the meantime? He may let you shower him instead of getting in the tub. Or, he may step into a bubble bath. Try switching from an after-dinner bath to a breakfast-time bath. With time, and a few dozen sponge baths, he'll get over it.

TIP

290

Doggie Decisions

Taking on a pet is only about 30 percent as involved as taking on another child.

Some pets are better than others, but let's look at the general principles as applied to a doggie:

- Do you have the time and room? Until your lil' tyke is old enough to feed and walk Fido, the job will fall to Mom or Dad. And if there's no room to house or walk the dog, forget it.
- Is your child a good match, temperamentally, for *any* dog? A shy, tentative fifteen-month-old who is chronically phobic (loud noises, strangers) may not be at the right developmental moment.
- Can you find a breed that fits in with your family?
- Can you handle a rambunctious puppy *and* a rambunctious one-year-old?

Go to the neighborhood pet store or the animal shelter to seek answers. The folks there advocate for pets as much as you do for your child.

TIP

291

Other Pet Possibilities

Besides dogs, as far as other furry friends go:

- Cats: Tread carefully. Felines tend toward independence more than canines and may interact poorly with an unpredictable toddler. Getting a kitten may allow the two to grow up together happily, but success is not guaranteed. And in these times of runaway allergy, it's worth noting that cat hair and dander is far more allergenic than dog hair.
- Gerbils, hamsters: Far easier choices and far more contained, but at the price of less interaction and emotional interplay than you'd have with dogs or cats. This need not be a negative.
- Birds, fish: We're receding, ontologically, far away from primates. You can stare at these pets and observe behavior.
- Insects, larvae: Well now I'm just having a little fun with you. We all know that people don't have insects as pets; insects have *us* as pets . . .

Go to Preschool

Unless your child's preschool is unusually—and perhaps unnecessarily—restrictive, set aside a few hours every week or two to be classroom mommy. Serve lunch. Read a book to the gang. Chaperone a field trip. Most teachers welcome the fresh energy and variety.

Parents who involve themselves in their very young children's lives find themselves closer to the friends and the issues their children struggle with as they grow older, up, and away. Nor are you likely to be blind-sided by a report: "Shayna's not making friends," or, "Ethan tunes out of sport activities."

Involving yourself in his preschool is a far better way to keep in touch with his life away from home than a Web-cam.

TIP

293

Germ Warfare

Children, like dogs, find nothing objectionable about sparklingly clear toilet-bowl water. Their grasp of the germ theory of disease is more suited to, say, early Renaissance than Wired Age.

Can he actually get sick from drinking toilet-bowl water? Well, maybe. It breeds bacteria, but it doesn't stand for very long before someone flushes it. If Dad has an intestinal flu, however, the odds go up.

But the world is also full of harmless, nonpathogenic bacteria. Even if your toddler drinks a bowlful, he probably won't get sick. The best ways to limit a child's exposure to germs are simple and few.

- Wash hands frequently, especially after he's played in a puddle, with other runny-nosed children, or after a visit to a place where lots of other kids play.
- Wipe down the changing table frequently. Clorox-soaked towelettes are a good choice.
- Clean the humidifier two or three times a month.
- Keep the toilet lid down.

TIP

294

Drooling

L ike the mixed bag of causes for stomachache, the variety of causes for drooling range from the innocent to the critical.

A child who is suddenly drooling, thrashing about, and turning blue has a blocked airway. Often a swallowed toy part or piece of food is responsible. An infection known as epiglottitis used to cause a similar picture to develop over the course of hours, but has been vaccinated out of existence.

Less serious causes of drooling, now that we've gotten the dire stuff out of the way, include teething and mouth sores. When a toddler's molars come in, the sore gums and general discomfort level cause the salivary glands to work overtime, and she'll leave little puddles in her wake.

In winter and summer, certain viruses making the rounds cause mouth sores, and this, too, causes overproduction of saliva. Every now and then (more so in adults and older children), a piece of food blocking the esophagus leaves swallowed saliva no place to go but back up. The number one food that obstructs the esophagus? Poorly chewed steak.

TIP

Paleness

Children who appear "pale" to their parents usually aren't. Pallor is lack of color from blood, so the concern is over anemia; doctors look inside the gums and eyelids, not cheeks and forehead, for a more accurate reading. These "mucous membranes" get their pink color from blood vessels underneath the surface. If properly pink, the pallor isn't anemia.

In anemia advanced enough to cause true pallor, there is such a short oxygen supply that the child is fatigued—and his heart works overtime to make the blood pull double duty. Iron-containing vitamins resolve this kind of pallor/anemia.

Sometimes, a minor viral infection causes a transient lowering of the bone marrow's ability to produce blood cells. The blood count usually snaps back pretty quickly, with no lasting harm.

The most deadly, though fortunately rare, cause of sudden pallor is leukemia. The bone marrow cannot produce normal red or white blood cells, leading to anemia and increased susceptibility to infection. The distinctive bruising in leukemia appears all over, including unusual places such as over the stomach or groin, or on the lips.

TIP

296

Lethargic vs. Droopy

The term "lethargy" is a red alert to a doctor, so please be very specific. True lethargy, to me, is generalized weakness and unarousability bordering on coma. As a parent, "lethargy" may just mean droopy, lackluster, sad, or cranky.

Droopy is common, lethargy is mercifully rare. Children with colds or other minor viral syndromes are droopy and unhappy. They have little of their usual energy but can be roused to drink enough fluids to keep them going. Kids may sleep more, but they're not overly sleepy when awake. They're just cranky and miserable.

Dehydration from diarrhea, vomiting, or inadequate drinking also leads to droopiness, but usually the ability to wake up isn't affected.

When a lethargic child comes to the ER, a flurry of activity ensues, often culminating in a tube being placed in the throat and a needle in the back to rule out meningitis. Other conditions that cause true lethargy include severe infections (besides meningitis), serious head injury, serious poisoning, acute kidney or liver failure, or a prolonged seizure. (In the immediate aftermath of a brief seizure, the lethargy is also quite brief).

Please: Be specific and choose your terms carefully.

TIP

297

Not-So-Stupid Food Trick

No self-respecting kid (and even fewer adults) voluntarily eats a bowl full of spinach, but don't take rejection as a sign of rejection. Spinach is a good source of iron, calcium, vitamins, and fiber. Put it into the food processor and turn it into micro particles; then add it to a macaroni-and-cheese lunch. You need not overwhelm them with the green stuff, either. A little bit every day or two will keep the nutrients coming in nicely. This works for broccoli, too. Hide 'em in pasta sauce. Put them on a pizza.

Sit down and share a bowl (or a slice) with him. If you eat it, he'll eat it.

TIP

298

Fab Four Tip

With songs like "Help!" and "A Hard Day's Night," one might understandably think that the Beatles had young children toddling around the recording studio. And perhaps their continued popularity has something to do with these sentiments any mom or dad can relate to.

Naaaah. But they may help those hard day's nights when hours and hours of twisting, shouting, and screaming leave you exhausted.

Think about the other early gems: "And I Love Her," "With Love From Me To You," "Revolution" (oops! wrong album!).

Sometimes all a meltdown needs is just a simple hug from Dad or Mom. No matter what the conniption was all about, there are a lot of restorative powers in a simple little snuggle. Hum her a song that was a hit before she was born—a song will make you feel good, too.

TIP

299

Comedy Classics

And now, pre-e-e-e-e-senting in the Mom-n-Pop Home Theater . . . Abbott and Costello's classic hit . . . *Who's On First?!*

Very little knowledge of baseball is required to keep a two-year-old in stitches with this classic comedy routine. The wordplay alone will crack him up. For scripts, go to any bookstore with a decent humor section and find a compendium (I recommend Novak and Waldok's *Big Book of New American Humor*) or type in the name of your favorite comedian or routine in a Web search engine. Monty Python sites abound, and though some of the humor may not be appropriate, the scripts make for some good, old-fashioned read-aloud fun.

TIP

300

The Good Dad

The good dad is a proactive dad. The good dad does not "baby-sit" for his children. The good dad is not always the good guy. The good dad is a father

In order to be a dad, accept your role as a constant presence, subject to the same demands as a mom. It's not an adjunct, hobby, or part-time gig. The responsibility of being a provider is but one factor in that relationship. You're also a person from whom they will learn (and imitate) behavior, values, and what to say when stuff breaks. You have no excuse to be any less of a parent.

Now that we have the ground rules established, let's play ball: Give the time-out when he's breaking things, hitting, and otherwise testing the waters. Clean the diaper in the middle of the night. Mediate disputes. You know—get your hands dirty.

TIP

301

Dads and Discipline

Dads have to develop their own discipline style. Set limits for tolerated and not-tolerated behavior, and be in sync with Mom on this. Nothing fosters chaos faster than conflicting sets of rules under a single roof.

Just because you miss him for many hours in the day, your son won't be automatically on his best behavior in the few hours when you're home and he's awake. In fact, you may get only the bad stuff at the tail end of his day, when his batteries run low and you're not in the greatest mood, either.

Don't pawn off the responsibility of intervening when he does something wrong. Showing off by spilling a cup to make a hellacious mess isn't tolerated by Mom, so you're not going to let him get away with it either (even if it is a little funny). Time for a time-out. If he discovers he can play Dad off against Mom you'll have a medieval monster in no time. This kind of behavior gets old, fast.

TIP

302

Dad Day

The good dad takes a mental health day off from work once in a while. Think of it as a reverse sick day. Go to a museum or zoo. Host a play date. Get acquainted with the morning, lunch, and afternoon child, and he or she may appreciate you in a whole new light, too.

Pack the lunch, the snack, the change of diaper, the change of clothing (just in case), and a few extra snacks and toys for the trip. Weekends just don't cut it—there's a whole separate mentality and set of routines for weekdays. The stores and museums are a lot less crowded on a weekday, too. Plus, on a weekend, you can cheat and ask Mom to "help" you get all the *stuff* together. Every once in a while, to appreciate Mom and your child better, it ought to be all on you.

Dad Night

Give Mom a night off. Let her have a play date minus kids. Kiss Mom bye-bye for the evening; then, take over. Dinner, brushing teeth, and bed. Fight the battles, clean the messes, extinguish brushfires. After their calming bath, play games and read books. Offer a final snack, make sure teeth are brushed. Don't make it a special night for the kids. Give the five-minutes-'til-bedtime warning, and remind them again with one minute to go. Then, lights out. No compromise. In other words, keep to the routine. Tell them Mommy will give them a kiss when she comes home. A last drink of water. No more stories.

Once they're asleep, you can relax and bask in the pleasure of having given Mom a well-deserved break.

TIP

304

Time to Go: The Bottle

Get rid of every bottle in the house once he learns to drink from a cup—and don't let bottles back in. Stock up on a generous variety of sipper cups. And even though you may get tears and tantrums at thirteen or fourteen months, it's nothing compared to the rage you'll encounter from an eighteen- to twenty-four-month-old.

Here's the carrot: Appetites are down after about the first birthday. Take advantage of eating and drinking less.

Here's the stick: Drinking from a bottle is linked to ear infections (from drinking while lying down), diarrhea (from excess juice), and tooth decay (from both).

If he asks where all the bottles went, tell him that robbers (or something less fearsome, perhaps, like fairies) must have come in during the night and stolen them all. The pleasure of shopping for and selecting new sippy cups can be part of the fun.

TIP

305

Time to Go: The Pacifier

When it comes right down to it, there's nothing clearly *wrong* with a toddler's using a pacifier. But I don't think there's anything clearly *right* about it, either. Sooner or later it's got to go, and sooner is always less of a battle than later.

Like kissing the bottle farewell, it emphasizes to your child he's growing up. He's no longer a baby. This may be important if a new baby is on the way, and keeping track of pacifiers becomes an issue.

Furthermore, sticking binky in his mouth makes it more difficult to express himself. It certainly makes it harder to understand him. If you sense it is inhibiting language development, make it a high priority to wean him. Limit the amount of time he has the pacifier, begin restricting it to home and certain times of the day. When he's sleepy, hungry, or acting up are the *wrong* times to give in. He'll never give it up if it's a crutch at stress times. Let him use his bankie, instead.

TIP

306

Teaching Good Food Habits

I'm not going to say it's easy to instill good nutritional habits in your children, but it's not terribly hard, either. If you've been good until the first birthday, you've made a great start already. A child's palate becomes accustomed to what it tastes day in and day out. By limiting the salt shaker, the butter dish, and the juice bottle, you've achieved plenty. When a couple of fruits are his only snack choice, he'll pick one and be satisfied. Drinking skim milk (after age two) becomes the normal milk. Ban sugar-coated cereals. The less they see *junk* now, the less they'll *crave* it later. Indulge, perhaps, but yearn for it? Maybe not.

Learn what you can about nutrition. Most books try to sugar-coat the technical stuff, but some are more easily digestible. The American Academy of Pediatrics' *Guide to Your Child's Nutrition* is informative and real-life helpful; somewhat more fun is *Feeding Your Child for Lifelong Health* (Susan Roberts et al., Bantam Books, 1999).

TIP

307

Nutrition: Healthy Snacks

Want to be the envy of your mommy group? You can, but it takes the concentration of a Jedi. Here's what to pull out for snack time:

- Pretzels, not chips: salt, but no fat.
- Soft dried fruit, not candy: sweet enough for a snack, with complex carbs a-plenty
- Veggie strips: carrots, cukes, peppers for dipping in plain yogurt
- Fresh fruit for dipping in frozen yogurt
- Tofu-based ice cream
- Say "No" to juice, juice, juice after the cup-a-day allotment. If they're thirsty, water or skim milk are best.
- Whole-grain and fruit "breakfast bars" or muffins, not cookies

Instead of letting the other women envy you, make a bargain. All the moms can choose snacks from this list so the kids won't fight over the food. Then the grownups can fight the good improve-your-own-diet fight together instead of alone.

TIP

308

Nutrition: Fiber Foods

Consider fiber. Fiber keeps bowels regular, and over a lifetime it may cut the risk of colon cancer way, way down. It also keeps the heart healthy. And it's not all that yucky, either. Make a veggie chili: beans and peas galore! If you can get over your unfounded bias against prunes and dried fruit, you'll open up a whole grocery aisle full of food for meals and snacks.

At breakfast time, fiber should rule. Bran muffins, whole grain bread or "breakfast bars."

For older kids, popcorn (minus butter, salt) is about as healthy as a snack food gets. Be careful with younger kids: There is a choking hazard if it's swallowed whole, or if kernels get into the bowl.

TIP

309

Nutrition News on the Net

You won't get objective information on nutrition just anywhere. Assuming that the Internet still exists by the time this chunky volume makes its way into print, I'd guess that some of the following Web sites might still exist, too.

In general, universities and hospitals are a safe bet. Tops on my list is *www.kidshealth.org*. Good content, good links, good recipes. Four stars. Also, have a look at *http://ificinfo.health.org*, the Web site of the International Food Information Council (IFIC). They're a nonprofit science-health watchdog organization. Newsy, yes, and more wonky than fun, but trustworthy.

I'd love to say the wholesome sounding Family Food Zone (*www.familyfoodzone.com*) is a great site, but it's from the dairy industry. Take a look at their recipe for, um, "Festive Butter Mints" and you'll see why you can't trust someone with a product to sell.

TIP

310

Lies and Lying

There are lies, damned lies, statistics, and "I didn't break it." The simple misstatement of fact, and the torrent of similar misrepresentations that follow, have a number of roots.

- Memory lapse: By the time you discover a misdeed, he may not remember he was responsible.
- Imaginary friends did it: Cause and effect are only fleetingly related. He may honestly have turned his wishes into "truth."
- Denial: He may not want to pay the consequence, so he'll insist that he didn't do it.

Give him a way to save face: "I know you didn't mean to break the glass, but I've told you before not to put it so close to the edge of the table." When he nods in acknowledgment, he's confessing. Don't push it any further. "I would like you to help me clean this up, and I appreciate you not lying about it." Another nod. You're well on the way to having an honest child.

TIP

311

Childproofing: Streets

Here's the *Toddler's Guide to Street Smarts:*

- Look left and right. Make this a very big deal. Because it is a big deal.
- Always go with an adult and always hold hands.
- Driveways are hazards. You may be tipped off by the rumble of a garage door opening, but you may not hear the incoming minivan.
- Pets: Fences may be broken, a leash may be held too lightly. If a doggie gets loose, don't tease the doggie and the doggie won't lunge at you.

TIP

312

Childproofing: Glass Doors

It's easy to overlook the invisible.

No, this is not a famous line of Yogi Berra's. I've encountered my fair share of victims in the ER who accidentally collided with a plate-glass door with results ranging from minimal to, well, keeping the plastic surgeon busy.

Glass doors are usually less of a hazard to household members than to strangers and visitors who don't have the unseen hazard on their radar.

Place stickers or other decorations on plate-glass doors to avoid disasters. The same goes for glass tabletops, a home item ill advised for families with young children anyway.

TIP

313

Poison 1

Toxins come in solids, liquids, and gases. Beware of the following:

- Visiting grandparents bring medications that don't have child-proof caps.
- Vitamins and Tylenol: Both iron (in vitamins) and acetaminophen (Tylenol) can cause serious toxicity or death.
- Caustic detergents and insecticides are often poured into smaller, "handier" jugs. How would your two-year-old know the stuff he finds in the garage isn't soda?
- Alcohols are toxic. Rubbing alcohol, paint remover, and antifreeze are all dangerous, and so is store-bought liquor—it can cause coma, convulsion, and death.
- In winter, think carbon monoxide (CO) and gas leaks. Gas has a characteristic smell, but CO is odorless and colorless. The symptoms (headaches, dizziness, nausea, and vomiting) are easy to mistake for flu and food poisoning.

TIP

The Web site for the American Association of Poison Control Centers (*www.aapcc.org*) has the best info on poisoning.

Poison 2

Here's what to do when a poisoning occurs, as recommended by the Poison Control Centers of America:

1. First, remain calm.
2. Call the Poison Control Center and have the following information ready:
   - Child's condition (breathing hard, vomiting, sleepy, unarousable . . .)
   - Exact product name and ingredients (It'll help identify the active chemicals.)
   - How much of the product was taken (a mouthful, a swallow from a half-full, four-ounce bottle)
   - Time of the poisoning, even if you can only guess "He went down for a nap an hour ago, and I saw him five seconds ago with the pill on his lips."
   - Your name and phone number
   - Child's age and weight
3. They'll tell you what to do next. Ipecac is used rarely these days, and you're likely to be told either not to worry or to go to the ER.
4. Be prepared to give first aid if necessary.

Stuck Heads

Keep your head to save his. Paramedics don't really need calls from a frantic parent whose child's head has mysteriously popped between the slats of a railing and now can't come out. This is an easy call that you can solve.

It's not uncommon: little heads gradually become big heads. The nothin'-sized noggin that slipped in and out of the staircase rail one day turned out to be too big to go back out the way it went in.

Well, remember, what goes in must come out. What went through the bars to get stuck moments ago can go right back again to get unstuck. You have to turn and twist it a little, just like he did to get into this, but keep cool. Make it a game. You need his help. Your best shot: chin tucked in and head tilted slightly to one side. This may allow one temple to slide past the bar and then you're home free.

Remember, never force it.

TIP

316

Stuck Knees

Knees get stuck between crib slats all the time. Like a trapped head, this is a situation that brings on more hysteria and panic than necessary. And this situation is much easier to fix. A bent leg widens the knee, and this is the position it's sure to be trapped in. Just reach in and bring the foot out. This straightens out the knee and poof!—it should sail out as easily as it went in.

New Baby on the Way

The top ten list of things big brother or sister should know about the new baby baking away in your tummy:

1. She won't play until about five or six months.
2. She'll cry a lot.
3. She's not much fun. See 1 and 2 above.
4. She takes up almost all of Mommy's time.
5. She takes up almost all of Daddy's time.
6. Daddy's got to take care of Mommy who's taking care of the baby.
7. She's always going to be hungry.
8. She sleeps a lot, which means big brother has to be quiet all the time.
9. There are going to be all sorts of new rules.
10. Mommy and Daddy love you as much as they love her; nothing changes that. And in time you'll be able to play with and enjoy and love the baby as much as Mommy and Daddy do.

Kicking the New Baby

Hannah seems to have gotten over her I'm-a-baby-too phase, but now she's turned into a criminal. Every time she sees her baby sister she slaps her or pulls her hair.

And what kind of response does that get from you? If you get angry and send her to her room for a time-out, it doesn't help. In fact, Hannah seems to be pretty pleased with herself, since even though it was negative interest, she got your attention.

The fact is, Hannah is jealous and can't think of any other way to express it. Plus, she's also a little disappointed. Although you may have tried to prepare her, while you were pregnant, that a brand-new baby isn't fun for *months*, she may never have really gotten the message. So she's expressing frustration with a disappointing playmate—an infant sister.

Let her express feelings about the baby. Let her know some negative feelings are okay. Offer her positive ways to help that make her feel more involved, like helping with diapering or singing a song for the baby at naptime. She'll get it, eventually.

TIP

319

Two Babies on Your Hands?

When your toddler starts regressing by acting clingy and babyish when the new baby appears, it's your job to help her remember she's bigger and more grown-up.

The brutal truth is that your toddler has been dethroned.

Insist that she act like the big girl that she is, and reinforce it by refusing to respond to her when she lapses into baby talk or cries for no reason. She hasn't really regressed, which means losing an advanced behavior. She's just copying the baby's successful attention-getting strategy, which is all about crying and baby talk.

TIP

320

Sharing Territory with Baby

A long with some big-boy time carved out of each day, when the baby can't intrude on big brother's time, set aside a space where he can play all by himself, without fear of intrusion from the baby. No toys, no crawling, no diaper bag.

It's a two-way street. Create a toddler-free zone for baby, where your older child has to respect the baby's belongings: He can't go in and act like a baby, and he won't be allowed to "read" the baby's books.

Hopefully, after a week or two, he won't need this kind of artificial border patrolling, and he'll understand how to share territory.

TIP

321

Care Miles

Corporations have learned how to buy loyalty over the last twenty years by offering incremental rewards: air miles. What works in commerce might work at home. Try "Care Miles."

When the jealous toddler sibling of a new baby acts in a helpful or considerate way toward the still somewhat despised new arrival, give her some Care Miles. Let her trade them in for a big reward—an outing to a museum or Discovery Zone—when she's accumulated enough points. Remind her each day or week that she's five care miles away from her reward, and offer intermediate incentives.

It may not buy love, but it buys peace.

TIP

322

Books for Older Sibs of a New Baby

The art of coping with a new arrival is a central issue. Here are some books to help:

- *Julius, the Baby of the World* (Kevin Henkes): For ages 4–7. Jealousy, revenge, and intricate plots may sound more like what you find in *Othello* or *Macbeth*, but it's also how Lilly deals with the brand-new baby brother who has usurped her throne.

- *Waiting for Baby* (Harriet Ziefert and Emily Bolam): For ages 2–4. A boy pats Mommy's tummy and tells his new beta-version sibling how much he loves him and the fun they'll have. Sweet and tender, it's worth bringing out when he feels more like Lilly (see above).

- *And Baby Makes Four: Welcoming a Second Child into the Family* (Hilory Wagner): For grownups. Hey, maybe you could use a primer too, right?

TIP

Surviving Bad Days

The day is fast approaching when she's a beast from the moment her eyelids flutter open until you strong-arm her back into bed again eighteen hellish hours later. Many spilled cups, scattered toys, and broken items later, as you head to the tub for a long bath (extra *bubbles!*), the only way you'll find the silver lining is as follows:

Look for an excuse—no matter how minor—to praise her at some point in the day for some virtue she's demonstrated and lavish her with hugs and kisses. An opportunity *not* taken to smack baby brother. A wrong-shaped cookie she *didn't* have a tantrum over. A beautiful artwork created with only moderate mess.

What you'll be most pleased with, as you reflect back on it, is how good it felt to rally your positive attitude when you could just as easily have given in to the dark side. And as you step out of the bath into the comfy robe that awaits, you won't even remember the bad stuff.

TIP

324

Parenting Exercise: Acknowledge Mistakes

L earn from your mistakes. Unless you get a 100 on the parenting test, you're bound to trip up sometime and make a plain old boner of a mistake.

What's the exercise here? Simple. Own up to it (either to yourself or your son or daughter, whomever will benefit from the self-appraisal), acknowledge the mistake, and move on. Blowing your stack over a minor infraction is just the kind of thing that happens once in a while. Apologize: "Mommy got very angry and yelled. I shouldn't have let you alone with the open juice container in the first place."

That's it. Keep it simple. Don't wrack yourself with guilt. You've built up a repository of trust and confidence and he'll give you another chance. He'll still expect calm and reason from you rather than raised voices and fury.

And if, ultimately, your self-confidence is eroded by behaviors in yourself you don't like, get professional counseling. Parenting is hard. Don't do it all on your own.

TIP

Parenting Exercise: The United Front

Test scenario: He toddles up, big, watery eyes begging to watch that video he's been asking for all day long. You say no. For whatever reason. No is no. Then, out of sight, he goes to Dad. Same big watery eyes, chin a-quiver, even more visible pain as he asks to watch the video.

Been there, right? Don't let Dad offer the big rewards Mom has been holding out on all day. Let's just say Dad got home from a trip to the coast and wants to be Santa-for-a-night. It's not fair to Mom if Dad gets to be the good guy all the time, and it's certainly not a good idea for Dad, in the long run, to be the patsy.

Even before your children hit you with pop-quizzes and parenting tests, have your common, united policy in place. If Mom or Dad said no, it's no. And don't get tricked: If he doesn't *tell* you Mom or Dad already said no, turn off the video or withdraw the treat once you find you've been conned.

TIP

326

Fun with Food Coloring

I'm always willing to stoop to new lows to try to outsmart a two-year-old. This is a cheap trick, but to get a few more mouthfuls per meal into a picky eater use a splash of food coloring: Green Eggs and Ham! (This, of course, is for non-Kosher families only.) How about "Blue Monday"? Add a few drops to waffles, cereal, even the milk!

Then dress her up in tie-dye and make sure you've got the Tylenol handy for the visual assault.

TIP

327

Sweet Rewards

A long-term incentive program that even a toddler can understand: a variant of the jellybean wedding jar.

For each desired behavior, especially ones that you are trying to encourage or habits you are trying to discourage, put a jellybean in a jar. For each misdeed, a jellybean comes out.

At the end of a week he gets to eat them. The better the behavior, the bigger the treat.

You never heard of a jellybean wedding jar? Every time you make love in the first year of your marriage, you put a jellybean in a special wedding jar. Every time you make love *after* the first year of marriage you take one out. According to legend, no one has ever emptied out the jar . . .

Tearless Hair Washing

She's two and a half, refuses to get her hair cut, and turns into a wild beast when you wash it. She also *never* lets you brush it, so it's a tangled mess all the time.

Try putting a washcloth on her face to avoid getting soap in her eyes. And a tangle free shampoo might help. If you comb her out after it's dried a little, you'll have a little easier time of it.

Another tack is to try making a game of it by bringing in a mirror and making wacky designs in her hair when it is full of shampoo.

You may have to settle for washing it only every three or four days, but it's a start.

TIP

329

Alcohol-Proofing

There isn't anything wrong with a beer or shot of whiskey every now and then—if it's for *you*. But please, keep this stuff out of the reach of children. Alcohol can cause serious, if not deadly, poisoning in toddlers. A few mouthfuls of 80-proof hard liquor can put a twelve-month-old into a coma. Alcohol lowers blood sugar to the point where permanent brain damage can result. Short of that, the low blood sugar and the alcohol itself can provoke prolonged seizures.

If you've ever wanted to see a doctor sweat, just watch one try to figure out how to get a one-year-old's intractable seizures under control, because nothing seems to work.

So a little friendly advice: Keep the moonshine away from the hands and mouths of climbing, curious toddlers.

TIP

Tobacco-Free

To be politically sensitive, let me clearly state that I don't for a minute think that any of you reading this are purposely subjecting your charming children to cigarette smoke. Nope, not for a second; it's more likely neighbor Ted, it's Aunt Penny, it's Daddy's fishin' buddy, Buddy.

So here are the reasons why you should completely prohibit them to smoke in your home. All of the following refer to the influence of secondhand (or environmental) tobacco smoke:

- It's present in 40 percent of SIDS cases (for those with a new baby at home).
- It carries a 20 percent higher risk of pneumonia and bronchitis in kids under age five.
- The risk of ear infections goes up by 13 percent.
- Asthma is more severe and more likely to require medical intervention.
- The risk of fire hazard is harder to quantify, but it is real. This includes house fires and burns from cigarettes themselves.

TIP

Firearms Kill People

A gun in the home is a lethal danger. People kill each other during household fights, commit suicide, or unintentionally shoot themselves or each other far, *far* more than they kill or wound intruding criminals.

I don't care how many safeguards there are. There's always some time when the gun owner is cleaning it or checking it or doing something with it that opens the door to disaster.

As an ER doctor, each year I see at least one child dead, or near dead, from an accident at home involving a firearm: a twelve-year-old shot by his ten-year-old brother, a six-year-old shot by a nine-year-old, and the list goes on and on.

Like any responsible doctor, I hate guns. Guns are my natural enemy. Guns have no role where there are children.

Get rid of yours.

TIP

332

The Good Dad at Supper

Suppertime! Heed the call. Mom and Dad, get home for as many family dinners each week as you can. Choose your minimum, two or three, and take a serious pledge that if you *can't* make that, you'll reorder your priorities so you can keep the promise. A dedication to family dinnertime, family time that cannot be violated, lays the groundwork for the future. Dinner is a time to share the experiences of the day, to laugh, to recharge batteries. It's when the heavy stuff and the lighter stuff is aired out: We're going on a trip to the beach! Grandma's coming to visit!

And a few years down the road, you have this to look forward to: Your report card looked great! Your mom just got the big promotion she's been waiting for! You're marrying *him*?!

Make sure your colleagues know the depth of your family commitment. They'll envy, honor, and respect it. (Unless, of course, they are the type to take this opportunity to stab you in the back.)

TIP

333

The Good Dad at Work

Call home each day. Keep a promise to yourself to check in at least once while you're at work. This keeps you in tune with their daily schedule. Make it a point to call after a nap or during lunch and let your child hear your voice. My bet is it charges your batteries every bit as much as it is a treat for the little one, too. If the morning's activities included an art project, have it faxed to you. They'll know you're there—no matter where "there" is, and it keeps you a part of daily life, even if you don't get home until late at night.

TIP

334

Dad Pride

The words your child wants most to hear from you are these: "I'm proud of you!" So please be sure to say it, and say it often. I know you feel proud of your kid in a global sort of way. As a guilty-as-charged parent, you are, perhaps, lacking in regular expression of emotion to your spouse as well.

Be on the lookout for any little moment or accomplishment that can make you sing out your pride: sharing a toy nicely, finishing dinner, getting into PJs without a fuss. What your child internalizes by hearing praise repeatedly is the idea that he is a valued and capable kid. This is the foundation for self-worth and confidence he needs to take on the world as he grows. There's no better gift a parent can give than this.

TIP

Band-Aid Cure

Speaking as an ER doc as well as a father, I am intimately familiar with the pain game. Most tots who panic and howl at the first wave of pain from a boo-boo sustain a howling agitation and outrage long after the immediate shock subsides. Therefore, after a five-minute or so cry, distracting them from the fresh trauma goes a long, long way. Hence, Band-Aids. And doubly hence, offering a choice of two or three Band-Aids, each featuring a different look or character (Pokémon, Rugrats, or whoever is the current hero *du jour*), is the best medicine. Once the boo-boo is covered up, call "game on" and continue directing their energy elsewhere.

Out of sight, out of mind.

Kid Music 1

Children will listen to almost any music an adult does. Part of learning culture and heritage comes from identifying with Mom and Dad's taste in music. Unless your taste runs to bruisingly assaultive high-decibel punk or the edgiest avant-garde experimental noise, the tunes you listen to have some musical merit that your children can respond to. Thus, any music can be kids' music.

It's always easiest to start with plain vanilla. Simple tunes, simple melodies. Don't expect to like it, but kids really groove to the likes of Raffi; Sesame Street; Peter, Paul and Mary; and Barney.

And yes, most assuredly, you'll be held hostage to the one favorite tape or disc she'll want to hear over and over and over again.

When faced with a long car trip you can, with a little maneuvering, set up your toddler with a pair of headphones that won't fall off and spare yourself endless repetitions of *Puff* or the *Barney* song.

TIP

337

Kid Music 2

Take turns. When she refuses to listen to anything but the latest Disney soundtrack for the umpteenth time, stand your ground and claim your right to a little grownup music. It needn't even be your kind of music, but she doesn't have to know that. Go multicultural. Explore new tastes and discover something fresh that you'll both like:

- One of the all-time great a cappella groups, The Persuasions, have a kids' disc—*On the Good Ship Lollipop*.
- The *Charlie Brown* soundtrack. You can hear the piano now, can't you?
- Any *Best of Motown* disc: Did it ever get better, really, than Marvin Gaye, the Temptations, and Smokey Robinson?
- World music awaits. Start with the Gypsy Kings.
- Buckwheat Zydeco is the beaucoup sweetest sound from the Cajun world.
- Last, and certainly not least, indulge in the glorious Ladysmith Black Mambazo. You first heard them on Paul Simon's *Graceland*, and they've got so much more to offer.

Kid Vid 1

The Mouse certainly doesn't need the benefit of my recommendation, nor is Orlando going to suffer if I issue a challenge to raise your toddler Mickey-free. And although the great purple Jurassic one, Barney, convulses most parents to the point of madness, the kiddies do love the dude. You really can't argue with his embrace of values like cooperation, tolerance, and creativity. Then we have *Teletubbies*. One doesn't think of the English as irreparably drug addled, yet how else to explain the mesmerizing effect of *Teletubbies*? It's a magic ride for a two-year-old. The Teletubbies neither instill good values or sing sweet songs. They're just sorta . . . *weird*!

Sadly, video transformations of Dr. Seuss are meandering, lackluster affairs. Spend the time reading the book to your kids.

So what do kids really watch? Anything. Just be there alongside them to make it a shared activity, and experience the world along with them.

TIP

339

Kid Vid 2

Explore the back shelves of your local video store for some interesting finds:

- *The Little Rascals.* Not only are they still riotously funny, but they give a grainy, jerky glimpse of a world long departed. By this I mean the way kids acted and spoke, not just the small-town ambiance or the complete lack of electronics in daily life.
- Abbott and Costello, the Marx Brothers, Charlie Chaplin, Buster Keaton. All are masters of good old-fashioned G-rated sight gags and slapstick.
- An odd but inspired series, *There Goes a . . .* introduces children to social and civic engineering: an airplane, a race car, a train and, yes, even *There Goes a Garbage Truck.*

TIP

340

Kid Software

When a baby is old enough to move a mouse and click on a screen, she's maybe twelve months away from being able to reboot your hard drive and recover all your data after a crash. Twenty-four months away from designing her own viruses.

The pick of the lot, from an educational standpoint, is the JumpStart series. They start toddlers out right and take them all the way up through elementary school. They lay out puzzles for kids (with huge on-screen cursors) that hook them into learning letters, numbers, and concepts.

Sesame Street also offers some invitingly fun choices, as you might expect, particularly Elmo's various projects.

Falling short of the mark, alas, is Dr. Seuss (as he does in videos as well). The games and riffs on the master rate poorly next to his books' clean elegance. They do a fine job of introducing letters, numbers, abstract reasoning: How does one find green ham in the first place? And how did they get those train tracks to perch on such improbable geologic formations? But the software does not achieve the same wonderful clarity.

TIP

Vacations: Double Up

From now on, when planning a vacation, start thinking economies of scale. Take a second family along with you and spare your wallet. Take renting a beach house, for example: Sharing a large house is cheaper than a small house, and once there, you have a built-in babysitter (for at least one night) to take a break from the kids.

Even if your children are not already the best of friends, corralling a duo is generally more efficient than chasing after a lone toddler. And the struggle to entertain them is easier: two peas make for a good pod.

By the end of the trip, you'll have a new appreciation for your neighbors. At the very least, you'll know what they look like when they first stumble out of bed each morning.

TIP

342

Tub Tricks: Shower Instead

Upon achieving independence on two sturdy small feet, a little variety can be thrown into the bath-time routine by making it a shower instead. Why go through tub trauma?

It works best using a showerhead on a flexible hose, preferably one with a variety of settings just to keep her attention. Remember, this is a new experience for your girl, and she may go crazy for the sensation of water spraying her all over.

It's not for everyone. The whole-body tickle that delights some children may be too much of a sensory overload for others. If she cries, carries on, and bolts out of the tub, go back to bubble baths to provide variety.

TIP

343

Turn the Tables

Want a real test of your child's language skills? Act as irresponsibly as she does. Defy logic and expectations with a good turning of the tables.

Next time she's shrieking at her play-date friend, interrupt their battle with a loud, clear, "I'm going to take a nap while you fight over that toy. See you in three hours!"

Amazing, isn't it, how fast and clearly they understand Mom then? Odds are her response will be something on the order of, "Don't be ridiculous, Mom. We're fighting dangerously here *and* we're not behaving or taking turns nicely. How can you leave us when we're this close to a nuclear meltdown? You're always just thinking of *you!*"

Not, perhaps, in so many words, but this is the gist of it. Other usable lines to try:

- "You stay here and throw a tantrum, I'll be at the checkout counter. See ya!"
- "I'm hungry! You make *me* lunch today."
- "I'm sorry, were you shrieking at me? I was watching TV and wasn't paying attention."

TIP

344

Private Parts

What *do* you call those parts to a curious toddler? Their correct, anatomical names: Johnson and Lucinda? Not exactly.

When it comes to the temple of temples we know as our physical selves, don't beat around the bush. Give it to them straight.

Little Peter will say "penispenis*penis*" or "vaginavagina*vagina*" at the top of his lungs repeatedly, especially when stuffy old Mrs. Winnipissaukee comes to pay a visit. Even more mortifying is when your precious little Angelica makes up and repeats, as our beatific little Zoe did, for months on end, the expletive "tushy*vaGINA!*" It's okay. When they grow tired of this phase, they'll move on . . . to other, grosser habits.

TIP

345

Family Restaurant Follies

Nothing says "insanely out-of-control madness" like a family restaurant. Let's set aside, for the moment, fast-food joints like Wendy's, Popeye's, and the Golden Arches. You have a nice range of choices. A survey from *Parents* magazine found all of the following offered uniformly fast, friendly service:

- Outback Steak House: booths and dark lighting help contain the mayhem, the menu is equipped for both kids and grow'dups
- Applebee's, Ruby Tuesday: more variety and healthy choices than a steak place, but the bright setting and fewer booths may require more chasing and "keep-your-voices-*down*" episodes
- Chicken Out: a cross between a fast-food joint and honest restaurant, but with good, fresh food
- Next time you're in Maryland or Virginia, make your way to Ledo's Pizza for the zestiest tomato sauce and flakiest pizza crusts anywhere on the East Coast. A perfect alternative down at the shore: Grotto Pizza

TIP

Photo Tip: Capture Paradise

Back in the winter of 1968, our family went to Puerto Rico for a warm-weather getaway. I was ten, my brothers twelve and six. A fading photo in a recently discovered album showed the three of us clustered in our parents' arms against the backdrop of a resort hotel, with a bright blue pool in the foreground.

I only vaguely remember the trip, mainly for how my brothers conspired to lose me in the pinball arcade room (those were the days before interactive video games). What I remember not at all is that my parents conspired to lose us so they could spend an hour or two at the casino.

But I do recall the sharp loss I felt when I realized that, having just been back to the *same hotel* a year or two ago, my own family lost the opportunity to recreate the next generation's family portrait framed by the same grand old hotel.

Don't make the same mistake. Before going on a future outing, go through your family's old photo albums and see if there isn't some landmark to pose against. Photo digitizing being what it is today, you should be able to blow up (and clean up) the old photos to make for a duo worthy of framing.

TIP

Gender Bender

You ought not to be overly concerned about your child's fitting into his or her proper gender role for years to come. By two, most children are socialized to their gender, even though their play sometimes goes against stereotype. A boy who likes to sit his action figures down to the dinner or breakfast table. A girl who brandishes a sword and screams "Hiiiiiiiii-YAA!" (Okay, maybe she's been watching a little too much Xena.)

No pressure should be applied to get your son to act more like a boy. He doesn't really know what this means, and he's following his play instincts. Same for a girl: If she's a warrior at heart, telling her to play Pretty, Pretty Princess is an unrewarding, losing battle. For both of you.

By the time they hit first or second grade your children will definitely have distinct alliances to members of their own sex.

TIP

348

Work at Home 1

A number of career opportunities exist for parents to work at home: freelance writing, software development, arts and crafts for fun and profit. But keep this firmly in mind: The huge challenge you're taking on involves, in some part, making it seamless for your child.

A simple phone conversation with a client is a prime example. The first time your one-and-a-half-year-old interrupts an important conversation with "Poooo-oooo-ooopy diapy!" is cute. The second time it's a problem.

Either your client will have to understand the limitations you have or, when your son's a little older, he will have to respect the "I'm busy now" cues. A message on your answering machine should be completely straightforward: "I may be managing a mini-crisis with Mini-Me. I'll call you back as soon as I can. His naptime is usually [. . .] o'clock, which is a good time to call."

Work at Home 2: Resources

Here are some resources from folks who've walked the walk:

- Magazines: *Working Mother* is geared for exactly your niche. Many other parenting magazines, including *Parent*, *Child*, and *Baby*, have at least one regular columnist or feature article with helpful hints or unique perspectives.
- Books: *101 Best Home-Based Businesses for Women*, by Priscilla Huff, or *Mompreneurs: A Mother's Practical Step-By-Step Guide to Work-At-Home Success*, by Ellen H. Parlapiano, and Patricia Cobe. These (among others) give you the straight stuff: partitioning your time and energy, setting up a business plan, and getting the loans to start success stories.
- Web sites: *www.homeworkingmom.com* is a good place to start for general tips, resources, and sanity clauses. Workingwoman.com advertises itself as the businesswoman's network, and is useful for moms both in and out of the home.

TIP

350

Work at Home 3: Boundaries

When your job corrodes the boundaries between work and parenting, it's time to create a new perimeter guard.

- Turn the pager and answering machine off, stay away from the phone during family time.
- Redefine "crisis." Your money is not your life. If money, contracts, or opportunities are *always* on the line, your family has probably been pushed *over* the line. The crisis may turn out to be the lost opportunity to be home for your child's first steps.
- Set limits on work taken home. Set limits on colleagues' access to your child-care time.
- Make a firm commitment: any intrusion on off-limits time will be made up from work time.
- Don't be intimidated, and don't lose your job. Learn your rights as an employee and go legal if you've been discriminated against.

TIP

351

Work at Home 4:
Don't Get Conned

Scams abound. You've seen the signs: "Earn up to $100 an hour on your computer!" First, do a couple of reality checks; then do a consumer-fraud check.

You know better than to give your credit card number out before you're guaranteed of receiving a product or service. So don't pay an "enrollment" fee to make money. (Hey! Here's a great money making idea: Have people sign up with YOU to make money and charge them a lower "enrollment" fee!)

Second, call your local Chamber of Commerce or Better Business Bureau. Just because someone can afford to print a few signs or take out an ad in a newspaper does not mean they're legit. If you've been bilked, call the National Fraud Info Center Consumer Hotline at 1-800-876-7060 to get the authorities on the case. Someone who's new at this may be easy to track down and put out of commission ("Crime makes you stupid!"). Even the pros get nailed eventually by pulling the same *modus operandi* one time too often.

TIP

352

Business Trip Companion

Inoticed the revolution at an American
Association of Pediatricians meeting a few
years back: on-site child care. Well sure, I
thought, this is the American Academy of
Pediatrics and they're way ahead of the curve.

Taking the tot along on a business trip these
days is not such a stretch anymore. If you've got
just a one- or two-day affair, make it a joint treat.
Add a day or two onto the trip if it's a good
destination (meeting planners know where
attendees want to come), and make it a special
vacation. On the downside: more planning and
distractions from the business at hand, fewer
opportunities to schmooze and network at after-
hours dinners or breakfasts. A counterstrategy
to the downside: If you absolutely must meet
with that client for a meal, have him bring his
child along, too, and have your meeting at the
zoo or aquarium along with your kids.

Busy, important parents have never had it
so good.

TIP

Card Sharp

By age two and a half, a child has the fine motor skills to hold a hand of cards and the language-behavioral skills to play some simple, classic games. With a little help every now and then, that is. Best games? Old Maid and Go Fish. Once she's learned the basics, a variety of card sets make it easy for her to learn a "new" game, such as Sesame Street, Mickey Mouse, or Barney cards.

If she has a true aptitude for the cards, move up through gin rummy and blackjack so that you can teach her the finer points of doubling down and the dealer draw on fifteen. How soon is too soon for Atlantic City?

Toothless Wonder

Teeth don't always debut by the first birthday. What to do, what to do? Nothing.

The first front teeth that appear top and bottom help to tear food, not chew. The solid gums, with nascent teeth just below the surface, do the chewing just fine. And most one-year-olds wouldn't even really know what to do with a food item—say, an apple—that does require "biting," so you'll be cutting it down anyway. For the late bloomer, you can continue to provide a full, unedited diet.

There are no long-term implications. If no teeth erupt by fifteen months, a visit to the pediatric or family dentist may be needed to get X-rays. They don't cut gums open to allow teeth out (how barbaric!) and rarely is a disorder uncovered whereby the teeth just aren't forming normally. (That's more on the order of one in a million.)

TIP

355

Where's the Bankie?

Where would you be without your Palm Pilot? Hobnaddled, as the Brits say. And that's just a tenth as desperately heartbroken as your two-year-old is when his bankie gets left behind somewhere.

Your darling son will, no doubt, react to the situation as hysterically as if it were the Cuban Missile Crisis. And what parent is unaffected by the depth of torment brought on by the loss of a loved one, even if it is a stinky, filthy rag?

What do you do when retracing steps through fourteen stores and three playmates' homes fails to retrieve it?

Console the poor thing, and expect a rough few days. He may find a backup (if he doesn't already have one waiting in the wings) and ultimately, he'll get over it.

If it's found, let him experience the delirious, overwhelming joy of getting it back.

It's a security blanket. He loves it, and sooner or later he will outgrow it.

TIP

356

Street Smarts: Animal Friends

Whether he's Fearless Frankie or Tentative Tommy, your child should have street smarts about furry friends he'll encounter:

- Don't tease. Petting is fine when Mommy or Daddy is supervising, but playing with a dog on a leash should be done only with the owner's permission.
- A growling dog, an arched-back kitty are warning signs. Back away slowly, and ignore the animal thereafter.
- Let sleeping dogs lie. They may reflexively snap upon awaking.
- Don't pull on any tails.
- Don't offer food unless specifically invited to by the owner. Don't let the animal help itself to your child's snack or meal.
- Stay away from any creature that is not a dog or a cat.
- Know that rats are the fast ones with the long nasty tails.

TIP

357

Free Free Weights

Close the curtains. Check the door to make sure it's firmly locked. Put the dog out.

Don't let *any*one see.

Get in your sweats and go to it: use your child as a free weight. She's twenty-five or thirty pounds to bench press and leg lift, or strap her on your back to do some push-ups. Go ahead, *try* it!

You won't get as many reps in as you would with an inert lump of metal, but it's so much more fun. Then, when she's used to exercising with you, get her dressed up in her own sweats and she'll pump along to your favorite workout tape with you.

Deny it if anyone tells you they thought they saw you doing something, you know . . . odd.

Road Trip Strategies

Before you're on the road again, toddler in tow, take a few minutes for advance planning. Some ideas, in case you've run out:

- Bring along a surprise. Favorite character decals (the clear plastic kind that peel on and off easily, not the perma-stickers that require an Act of Congress to remove).
- Pack a snack he's not normally allowed at home. The more carb-loaded it is (muffins, high-fiber bread), the better the odds he'll drop off to sleep while digesting it.
- Build up anticipation for the snack or present. Pick a landmark (when we get to the Tallahassee Bridge, the sign with the upside-down cow . . .) and promise he'll get it five minutes after that.
- Give him a map and crayons, and let him trace a route (real or imaginary).

TIP

359

More Road Trip Strategies

Okay, you've been there, done that, but now you have to go back there again. I've racked my brains to come up with a few more goodies:

- Stop-n-Stretch Fire Drill. Run around the car twice, hop around it, then hop around it on the other foot.
- Give him a cheap disposable camera to make his own travel scrapbook. You'll be surprised at the occasional gem that shows up.
- Make a mess. Give him a few sheets of scrap paper ahead of time. On a given signal (a red light, a blue truck, an airplane overhead) he gets to shred the paper into a million pieces.
- Clean the mess up at the end of the trip. Him. Not you.
- Unravel an old cassette tape. You must have *something* lying around that you won't ever listen to again (I'm thinking *Frampton Comes Alive*, here, and some '80s hair bands) and let him unravel to his heart's content. Look, you have to clean up the car afterward anyway, right?

TIP

360

Crisis Management on Road Trips

Every prolonged car trip should be approached with the same question in mind: What do I do if she throws up? The following are essentials for peace of mind and limiting any sort of catastrophe:

- Have wipes and more wipes, for the upholstery (Clorox wipes) and for her.
- Bring along a change of clothes, extra diapers.
- Pack an emergency kit: garbage bags, paper towels, even a hand-held vacuum.
- Have an extra water bottle. Formula or OJ are no good for an upset tummy.
- Program your cell phone with the pediatrician's number.
- Cheerios. These are an appropriate food no matter what.

TIP

361

Time-In vs. Time-Out

Not every child responds to time-out. A different way to discipline willful, oppositional behaviors is a "time-in" approach. Start by asking; then act.

But first ask yourself what the transgression involves: Safety? Attitude? Then ask her the appropriate questions: What happened? Do we have rules about hitting and taking turns . . . ? The trick is to ask without the implicit threat of punishment. You want her to explain her actions, and begin to think about them. You don't want her to fear reprisal.

The next step is action, Jackson.

Take away the thrown toy, or the favorite juice bottle that has just been splattered. Put it away until she's earned it back. Put yourself into the play date or game if turn-taking is being violated. Squash misbehaviors, but keep the activity going (assuming, for the moment, that exhaustion and naptime are not factors).

The next two steps are just ahead.

TIP

362

How to Do Time-In

Time-in is labor-intensive. After asking and acting, attend and amend.

Attend to the play situation that led to the nasty, unsafe, or acting-out episode. Watch out for the friend not playing fairly or antagonizing your child. Look at your own attitude and ask yourself if you've been consistent in enforcing the rules. Maybe the hosting mom has a different set of rules and priorities that you need to iron out.

Finally, negotiate through the wreckage to make amends. If your little girl has torn her friend's book she needs to get her a new one. Restart a game no matter who was winning and how close it was to the end.

This all requires more work than hollering time-out and chilling until the situation resumes again. But it may get you a lot farther, further down the road.

How to Talk to a Toddler

The blessed moment will arrive, sometime around a year and a half, when you can really talk to your toddler—and communicate. Talking to a toddler is distinctly different than cooing to a baby, or gushing about your baby to your friends and loved ones.

Communicate effectively. Forsake the baby-talk. At mealtime, tell her "it's time to eat your noodles" instead of "baby wan noo-noo?" Just as a non-English speaker won't understand you when you say, "Foot! Get OFF!" yelling and mangling your syntax isn't going to advance your child's grasp of proper English, either. Stick to normal (and correct) grammar: "Please get off my foot."

Correct her on the big words. Saying "re-fridg-idator" or "cops-ikle" is cute, and has a big, big place in her overall adorableness, but make an effort to teach correct pronunciation of the longer words. She'll be more successful scholastically and socially if she grows up knowing how to call things by their true name.

TIP

364

On to Childhood

The moment—a date, an hour, a vivid second—your baby is no longer a baby, the time she took her first hesitant step is forever recorded in your mind's eye. But there is no such instant to mark the transition from being a toddler to being, well, a *kid*.

Notable events contend for that title: perhaps the last diaper, striking the crib, or retiring the stroller. Yet none of these really suffice. Somewhere along the way, you relied on her to help you in some specific way and she came through. Or she helped put the groceries away because she saw you needed the help. Or you picked up the phone—and it was for her. And in a flash of recognition, you feel deep inside, deep down, the distance traveled, the gains made, the sweet reflection of early memories drifting farther and farther into a golden haze of a past, out of reach but for the few mementos snatched along the way. 🌰

Index

365 TV-Free Activities
You Can do with Your Child
Steve and Ruth Bennett

If you're like many parents today, you probably think that your children should watch less television. You'd probably like to replace some of your kid's TV viewing with quality family time, too. This book can help you achieve both goals by showing

Trade paperback, $7.95
ISBN: 1-55850-585-7
Ages 2 and up

you games and activities that require little or no preparation, yet provide hours of entertainment and play that might otherwise be spent in front of the tube. With a year's worth of TV-free activities in hand, you can confidently offer your kids exciting alternatives to programming of questionable value and an endless stream of advertising.

365 Tips for Baby's First Year

Julian Orenstein, M.D.

New parents everywhere are looking for quick advice for life's littlest challenge: their new baby. In *365 Tips for Baby's First Year*, Dr. Julian Orenstein provides fast answers to all of the most basic questions. Covering the full range of issues

Trade paperback, $7.95
ISBN: 1-58062-296-8

from serious medical conditions to regular discomfort, boredom to anxiety, feeding and sleeping, and much more, this illustrated reference is perfect for new parents or caregivers.